This book is dedicated to:

Ryan, your memory will live
on in my heart and soul

Rose, who introduced me to Mrs. H

Ted, who came up with the book title

Chapter 1

"Where are you" the text message read. It was a regular and anticipated message which we receive every week at 6.30 pm as we walk from our apartment on Poniente Beach in Benidorm to the old town to meet everyone for Monday Club at Brief Encounter, a small bar owned by Andy and Trevor. Where were we? In a small clothes shop where Jane or Mrs. H as she is known around the old town was looking at shirts to compliment her ever-increasing cowgirl collection. Mrs. H has a second sense that can spot a shirt, blouse, gypsy dress, or boots from several miles away and I am an unwilling participant in this daily ritual, like most husbands I nod, gesture, and make all the right noises to expedite the task in hand to get to the bar and sink a very cold pint.

Monday Club has become a tradition and club members rock up to Brief at 6.00 pm when the bar is opened by Kev who is married to Dan: the sender of the "where are you" message. Both are long term friends who used to own a late-night bar called 7th Heaven which was a den of smuttiness, debauchery and was bloody good fun, it also happened to be one of my local bars having been opposite my old apartment. Kev now works the bar, in Brief, welcoming the early punters whilst Dan helps with glass collecting, cleaning, and chatting to the customers. Monday club is a chance for locals to catch up, moan, laugh, and more importantly get pissed before they open their bars or go to work in one of the thousand-odd bars in Benidorm. On this day, the usual suspects are already there, Dennis the Enforcer who now in his autumn years has mellowed however be warned, he sits up in the Royal Box and when he nips out for a fag do not ever sit on his stool. Dennis comes across as a gentle and kind guy underneath his hat is the grim reaper who will break bones and grind them up to use in one of his fantastic meat pies; you have been warned. The boys from Bar Code will be there with their turbocharged shopping trolley, the trolley is something of beauty and reminds me of a sparkling 1980's XR3 with stripes and flames down the side; something of envy which both Trevor and Eddie guard like a new-born baby. Before you judge and mock let me explain the wisdom of a shopping trolley; Most people in Benidorm live in apartments and the daily or weekly trek to the local supermarket is an arduous journey, especially when you have litres of bottled water, milk, and veggies. Those in the know like the Bar Code boys invested in the daddy of shopping trolleys and we stand there at Monday club admiring this canvas beauty with sighs of admiration like Jeremy Clarkson does when he looks at a Bugatti on Top Gear.

As the sun goes down and a few pints later Briefs owner Andy shows his face, known as Shrek, he is a big lump of a man who despite appearances is a raving queen who is happily married to Anibal, a chef at Cava Aragonesa the tapas bar a couple of doors down. Andy, like all good landlords, spends the next few hours taking the piss out of all his punters and shoving extraordinarily large measures down all their throats. It is great to see the customer care course wasn't wasted on him.

So, Monday club is where I am now, but this story needs to be taken back a few years, a few characters, and a lot of bizarre moments. We need to go back to 2012 which is when I decided to make the move to Benidorm after several years of doing what the Americans call 'working for the man', I was feeling dissatisfied with my life and yearning for something more exciting. Like so many people I realised that getting up at the crack of dawn and coming home at 8 pm just to do the same thing wasn't pushing my buttons. Even the weekends had become the same tedious conversations; pubs had become boring with the same middle-aged guys moaning about their wives, jobs, children, and life. I could see the next 20 years of my life unfolding in front of me. God help me.

Having married young, fathering 2 boys, and then getting divorced in 2004 my life had followed a traditional path and now I was 45 years old and it was 2012; I needed to make changes. The sort of change I needed was a complete reinvention of my life, something that would give me new impetus and direction. For many of us, real change is something that normally involves relationships, work, or a house move; the problem with all of these is unless it moves you into a direction that challenges every part of you it is just transference and those issues that plague your soul just follow you. I have heard so many times you should move outside your comfort zone, look inside yourself and dig deep; I always thought this was a load of mumbo jumbo peddled by flaky yoga teachers who sit on top of mountains chanting, meditating, or some other weird spiritual nonsense. But I began to realise that it wasn't the mountain that mattered rather where the mountain was, it's easy to take the piss out of flaky yoga teachers but maybe they are on to something.

I knew that my move would be to Benidorm, this is a place I had visited since the early '80s, and whilst the usual sun, sea, and sand thoughts were appealing it was the community spirit that I liked. I know many people say "it's Blackpool with the sun" but I completely disagree with this, firstly and I apologize to anyone who lives in Blackpool, but Benidorm is nothing like it; it's cleaner, prettier, and has a culture that is nothing like the northwest of England. Most jokes and slurs about Benidorm come from people that have never been there and have only ever watched programmes on TV about the new town and all the drunken stag parties. When you tell someone, you are going on holiday to Benidorm, initially, they laugh and then they look at you and say with an irritating smirk "seriously???" Most people never see beyond the new town, they have never been to the old town and visited the incredible tapas bars, the wonderful restaurants, and more importantly, spent time with the gentle and friendly Spanish people that live and work in the resort. Benidorm has one huge advantage over other holiday resorts, it is a 12 month a year sunshine destination which is also a fully working town.

My life in Woking had been a mixture of work, chasing women, and looking after my teenage son Ryan. Work was running some guest houses that I owned with a mate and our esteemed guests were becoming odder, most were referred by the local council so you can surmise that we were not a classy joint. I had become tired of dealing with shit which included finding a dead body in a room, one of the guests tried to murder the neighbour and the local Russian gangsters visited me as they were unhappy that one of our satellite buildings was being used as a brothel unbeknown to me. When you are told by 2 big guys in black suits to "close your operation or else" you tend to take notice. Secretly, I was quite proud that they considered me a pimp and a threat to their operation; I had to impart the bad news to the 3 Somalian girls who lived in the house. A few days later I received a call from the local council who asked me if I had a room, I did, so a couple of hours later a young woman knocked on the door and I let her in. I gave her a cup of tea and explained the rules of the house. As I took a sip of my tea, I asked her what she did for a living and I was waiting for her to say that she was a waitress, shop worker, or something equally unglamorous; she looked straight at me and said, "I'm a dominatrix", I spat my tea all over her. We never got sweet old ladies, retired colonels, or young newlyweds; our guests were a little more colourful. The guest houses opened my eyes and ears to some of society's stranger elements, but they were lovely people, although I will draw the line at one particular guest. Early one morning there was a bang on the door whilst I was cooking breakfast, I rushed to answer it, who could be trashing on the door at 7 am? There stood 5 police officers who asked me if a particular gentleman was staying with us, I said yes, and they all went up the stairs and unnecessarily kicked in the gentleman's door and dragged him out of bed. He was put in the back of a police van and taken away, I was told by one officer he wouldn't be coming back so I then went to clear out his room and hidden under the wardrobe I found a big bag containing tens of thousands in cash. We held onto this bag and a few days later some very unsavoury and frightening looking guys turned up at the door, even more, menacing than the Russians they asked if we had found a bag in the bedroom, we happily handed it over and thankfully that was the end of the story.

Whilst I was dealing with Russian gangsters, Somalian prostitutes, and bags of dodgy cash I decided to get away for a few days, as it was January, and I couldn't be arsed to go too far I settled on Benidorm. Over the years I have travelled a fair amount and enjoyed the solitude of traveling alone, so nipping over to Spain for a few days was a blessing. I had booked into the Bahamas Hotel which upon arrival turned out to be more like the Isle of Dogs rather than the Bahamas; however, I didn't care as I was there to catch some winter sun, drink beer and hopefully pull some birds. I had a fantastic week and achieved all my aims and even came back with a suntan, but more importantly, I came back with an idea, I just needed to run it past my son Ryan

Ryan knew that I had itchy feet and when I got back, I said to Ryan that I had decided and although incredibly selfish I needed to do it. Ryan looked at me with both trepidation and a sense of excitement. I said to him "I have decided to move to Benidorm", I can't stand living here any longer and I need to change my life and follow my dreams. I was expecting Ryan to say something like "are you mad" or "what about me" but nope; he said, "when are we leaving"? My heart could have exploded at that moment and I said to him "as soon as we can get organised". Ryan jumped up, flew up the stairs, and started packing, that his excitement; I think like so many kids of his age they were lost and didn't want to grow up too quickly.

You would think that moving to a different country would be hard, but it is straight forward. I owned my own home in a highly desirable part of the southeast so renting it out was straightforward. We packed up clothes, tools, and personal bits into a dozen big boxes and the haulage company was booked to pick them up the following Friday; from the moment I told Ryan to the day we caught a flight, it was a dizzy 2 weeks.

The locals down my pub could not quite get their heads around it and raised the obvious questions, "why", "what will you do" etc etc but none of this fazed me or Ryan. I had booked a hotel for a couple of weeks and our belongings wouldn't arrive until the end of the month so plenty of time to find an apartment. As for what we were going to do, I had no idea and that excited me.

So, after a party at the local pub, the following day Ryan and I caught a flight to Alicante and our journey had begun. It is a strange feeling when you have a one-way ticket, unlike a holiday when you start counting down the days the moment you leave the house; for us, it was very liberating. We arrived in Benidorm in the afternoon and straight into the hotel, like most guys we threw our bags in and headed straight out for a few beers.

Our hotel was basic and traditionally Spanish with yellowy-brown pine furniture and squeaky beds, the balcony overlooked a residential street and there were no views apart from hanging washing and countless dogs barking on balconies.

I can't remember how I got talking to Irish Gerry but during the conversation, he told me that the apartment downstairs from him was available, it had 3 bedrooms and was centrally placed. Gerry kindly planned for us to see the apartment, which was located down the Alameda, a tree-lined boulevard in the old town with plenty of cafes and bars. The apartment was long and spacious with the usual issues one finds in Spanish property, the odd socket hanging out, a minute water heater, and a lightwell that looked like something out of a horror movie. For those that have never rented an apartment on the continent and don't know what a light well is, Apartments are built around a courtyard that provides light into the rear. When I say courtyard, I mean a concrete square where you hang your washing out on runners and peer into your neighbour's apartment, they are like wind tunnels in winter, and nothing can grow there as they are dark and damp.

I paid the compulsory 3 months' money and signed the contract which looked like something from Napoleonic times with stamps and wax seals and we were given the keys. Rents in Spain are cheap compared to the UK, we paid 450 Euros a month for this apartment and it included water, rates, and service charges. I of course had the biggest bedroom at the back, and Ryan had the one in the middle; our lounge overlooked the street which was always a hive of activity especially the bar opposite which is owned by a lovely Spanish woman who is apparently 'connected', mental note.........don't mess with the ginger-haired Spanish woman.

The apartment didn't come with a lift and we were on the 4th floor so hauling up bottles of water and gas was a major chore, but we loved it and we settled in quickly. Ryan started looking for a job in the new town and was offered a couple of bar jobs which he thought about but preferred to prop for a bar on the British square. For many people, props are irritating and can be seen hanging outside bars trying to coerce people in with the promise of free shots and cheap drinks. Whilst this can be irritating it is a vital part of many bars business and as many bars are not always on the main drag and rely on props to steer drinkers into their bars. Most props earn their money on results so next; you give a prop a hard time just remember that they pay their rent, feed themselves on the results they get.

I was trying to work out what I wanted to do, bar work didn't appeal to me and it lacked the challenge that I was searching for. We had been in Benidorm for 2 weeks and I spent a huge amount of time exploring all parts of the town and walked miles, something I have always enjoyed. Occasionally I would pop into a hotel bar in the old town and be mesmerized by how badly run the hotel was and the complete lack of service, something that is not unusual in Spain and bad service is all part of the culture, I was told that things move a lot slower and you just get used to it. The hotel was quaint and small but hadn't been refurbished since the 1970s and had that old wooden musky smell and a feel that continental bars have; it certainly felt like it was trapped in a time warp. The same old Spanish men would sit at the bar every day nursing a small beer or a cortado, the smell of strong Spanish cigarettes filled the bar and the occasional shout from the kitchen would indicate that something burnt was coming out. All the food that came out of the kitchen looked the same and was always swimming in oil, I even dared to try a traditional Valencian dish which consisted of chips and ham thrown into scrambled egg; the bucket of olive oil that came with it wasn't optional. English breakfasts were truly terrible and again eggs were cooked in olive oil, the whole plate had more calories than a family would eat in a week, it was by far the worst breakfast I had ever eaten.

People stayed at the Babylon not because of the beautiful surroundings of the old town, it was ridiculously cheap. There were a couple of worn outdated leather sofas in the bar with 2 aging ladies stuck to them, judging by their outfits I assumed they participated in the world's oldest profession, after seeing several gentleman callers take them upstairs over the day, I wasn't wrong in my assumption. The one redeeming factor that did help the Babylon was its location, Calle Alicante was the main thoroughfare through the old town and got lots of passing trade; it was also a well-known and established hotel.

Chapter 2

I had established that the Babylon offered nothing but bad service, terrible food, and a bar area that had peeling paint, prostitutes, and absolutely nothing that would attract the thousands of tourists that visited the old town every year. With this in mind, I saw an opportunity and at last found the challenge I was looking for. Was I crazy?

Within 2 weeks I had bought the lease for the Babylon and I was now officially a hotelier, a grand title considering that Pension Babylon as it was officially known as one of the worst hotels not just in the old town but in the whole of Benidorm; not a bad accolade considering there are approximately 200 hotels. Trip Advisor had various reviews with most starting with the words "truly dreadful", so it was clear that I would have some work to do.

Buying and running a business in Spain is nothing like the UK, for those that think it will be a walk in the park; think again. Spain operates 2 economies, an official one where you nip to the local bank and deposit cash with the hope that they won't lose it, and the ever-thriving black economy where cash is king and undeclared. Black money in Spain is a real issue and many deals are done under the table, a handshake, a few grunts, and a nod seal the deal, you also have to show some legitimacy, so a small percentage is declared. Whilst buying the hotel I had to deal with local lawyers known as 'Abogados' who traditionally have dingy smoke-filled offices which transport you back to the 1970s, very much like most things in Spain. As you enter you feel a real sense of foreboding, I am sure this is designed to intimidate and feel one with dread, it worked, and I was seriously nervous. I would get the nod and some garbled Spanish from the secretary who looked like she just got off the set of a 1970's sitcom to go into an office at the end of the corridor. There sat 5 men, all smoking and laughing, I get the feeling I was the butt of their joke, another stupid 'Guiri' a term used by the Spanish to describe a northern European tourist is about to lose his life savings. Behind a very grand desk sat a lawyer who was supposedly meant to represent me, although this is meaningless in a country where corruption is rife, opposite him sat the seller of the hotel along with his accountant and his lawyer; the other chap was an interpreter. When you buy a business in Spain and you are a foreigner the contract must be read out in both Spanish and ideally your native language, once you are satisfied with the wording money then changes hands. Counting out the money in small notes was a very strange feeling to me but a norm for these guys. The contract was then stamped and signed on each page; hands were shaken, and the hotel was mine; this was of course after a few extra thousand euros was shelled out by me for various bills that were due, and the standard payoffs to those in power.

The purchase was delayed by a week due to 'Banco I don't give a shit' losing my money which according to them was never transferred from the U.K. into my account. After a lot of screaming and shouting at the manager and showing him proof that Lloyds had transferred the money, he conceded that they didn't know where the money was but would investigate it. Spanish banks tend to slightly lapse when it comes to customers' money and although mine suddenly reappeared it was met with a shrug of the shoulders and no apology. For those of you that decide to move to Spain, get used to Spanish banks and their slower than slow approach to doing things. If you decide to pay your electricity bill at the bank, make sure you remember that this is done on a Thursday between 10 am and midday, any other time you will be met with a hurl of unintelligible negatives from the cashier, and they will carry on chatting with the old woman who just pushed in front of you. Beware of all old Spanish women, they are not just rude and have faces like a slapped arse, they will kick you, stamp on your feet, and barge you out the way to get in front of you. If you are unfortunate enough to be stuck behind them on the pavement it will become glaringly obvious that it is impossible to get past them as they walk 4 abreast and are oblivious to all that is around them, you have been warned.

When you have given up trying to pay your electricity bill at the bank you then try the automated service through the cashpoint machine, for those that don't have a command of the Spanish language, this is a traumatic and alcohol inducing process. If you opt for the English version, it directs you to the wrong page and cancels the transaction. The machine will read the barcode through a laser, but this only works if the sun isn't shining on it, in Spain where there is an average of 300 plus days of sun a year this can be a real issue. Should you succeed after several attempts in paying your electricity bill, after a lot of swearing you will walk away not only with a risk of a heart attack from the stress but also pockets full of change which your local bar owner will be happy to relieve you of as banks don't like giving change to businesses, albeit the change will be a mixture of small coppers that are completely useless and normally end up in a pot in your apartment later destined for the local dog charity.

With the keys to the Babylon in my hand, Ryan and I triumphantly walked back to the old town and stopped at Oliver's for a beer to celebrate. I must admit, I wasn't sure what to think; I had just bought the worst hotel in Benidorm. The cold beer was wonderful and at that moment Ryan and I felt invincible, we had no idea how we were going to turn the Babylon around, but I knew from running guest houses in the UK it couldn't be any worse, could it? I had had my fill of Russian gangsters, dead bodies, and neighbour murdering guests, although I did inherit 2 prostitutes when I bought the hotel.

I walked into the Babylon and was greeted by the manager appointed by the previous owner; I could tell immediately she wasn't happy with the sale and her position was venerable as she was to be moved to another hotel by her employer. As part of the deal, I inherited Gladys who was the cleaner, cook, and barmaid; she was a Chilean and had a very fiery temperament. Within 24 hours I had thrown the manager out of the hotel after she was rude to Ryan and ignored and dismissed him. She had lived in the hotel and chosen one of the best rooms for herself, when I say the best rooms I mean by location and views rather than décor which was awful. Her room was yet another tribute to the '70s with green flock everything and one of those disgusting shroud things that hang around the headboard, to say the room was kitsch is an understatement; it was repulsive. After going around all the rooms in detail it was clear that a lick of paint wasn't going to sort the rooms out; they needed a complete overhaul. The hotel consisted of 10 en-suite rooms and 5 with a shared bathroom, all looked like they had come out of a 1972 Thomas Cook brochure, although the wiring was far older and truly dangerous. I was even more amused at the size of the showers which were designed for anorexic dwarfs, getting in the shower was one thing, getting out was virtually impossible.

The bar downstairs had yellow pine cladding around the walls which reminded me of a Swedish sauna from a cheap horror film, all that was missing was a splatter of blood left by a clumsy serial killer. Off the bar was a kitchen separated by one of those bead curtains which made that awful noise every time someone went through it. Off the bar was a small opening that took you into the hotel reception area although this sounds grander than what it was, a piece of kitchen worktop fashioned into a reception desk, behind it was a damp musty cupboard which was used for guests' cases. The only thing that was clean and up to date was the toilets which had been completely refurbished a year previously, the ladies had one of 3 massive water boilers which supplied hot water to the hotel, this was right above the toilet so one had to crouch when doing one's ablutions. Despite the age of the bar and the old metal sliding doors, there was a certain charm about it, a non-conformity which most other hotels felt obliged to ignore and they spent tens of thousands trying to outdo each other.

At the top of the stairs was a roof terrace which was used by the odd guest for sunbathing, there were some old metal café tables, white plastic chairs, and some broken sun loungers, this was in addition to all the rubbish that had been dumped there over the years, specifically broken furniture, and mattresses. The views from the terrace were not amazing but they did give you a feel for the old town with terracotta roof tiles and a slight view of the sea. Like so many properties in Spain, the Babylon had been seriously neglected by its past owners and more so by the landlord who felt the need to skimp and save on all electrical, plumbing, and sewage.

Ryan and I set about working the bar and getting to know the locals, the bar attracted a steady flow of ex-pats and few old Spanish guys, being the first bar open in the old town it was popular with those looking for an early beer. From day one we met some lovely people, and many remain good friends to this day, some not so and others died off or just disappeared. The first few weeks were far trickier than I thought, I certainly didn't expect to be arguing with drug dealers, pimps, and prostitutes who had an arrangement with the old manager whereby rooms would be rented out by the hour. Being an unofficial pimp and being offered a cut for services rendered wasn't really where I wanted to be and reminded me of the big Russian guys who had paid me a visit in Woking.

The bar opened from 9 am until 2 am so Ryan and I had to work alternate shifts with most of mine being in the morning due to Ryan finding it hard to get out of his bed and me having to deal with deliveries etc. One of the first pieces of business I needed to deal with was getting the beer set up, an easy job one would think but not in Spain. I spoke to a couple of beer companies who said they would send someone around, they never turned up; so, after a bit more hassling, I got a time and date from one company; Thursday at 10.30 am. Thursday came and went, I ended up going to a British owned supplier who not only set up the pumps but also delivered on time. I still say to this day, if you want something done in Spain get a Brit or the Dutch to do it. 3 weeks later, on Thursday the original beer guy turned up at 10.30 am and said that we had a meeting, his words to me were "I never told you which Thursday".

Opening the bar in the mornings was a straightforward affair, turn the coffee machine on, run a couple of pints off to clear the lines, stock up on any bottles, etc, etc. One morning, however, this was 2 weeks after taking over the Babylon I turned up to find water gushing out the doors. When I opened the doors, the gush turned into a flood and the whole downstairs was under a foot of water. It transpired that during the night the mains pipe had burst, and half of Benidorm's freshwater had escaped through my doors, this was fixed fairly rapidly and a few weeks later I received a water bill for 33,000 Euros; after some wrangling, we managed to get this covered by the landlord's insurance... Phew.

Despite prostitutes, druggies, and floods, things started to settle down and we got into the swing of things, bookings for the hotel were non-existent due to the completely false accounts given by the previous owners so I spent time in the bar or painting the rooms. Our regulars would turf up most mornings as I opened the doors, and they would have their favourite stools and I could tell the time by them. Ronnie, an ex-pat who has been in Benidorm for over 20 years is a well-known face in the old town, a retired accountant he now spent his days drinking beer and chatting with the hotel guests when we had some. Ronnie also helped in the early days and became part of the furniture at the Babylon and was like family. We had Miguel an old Spanish guy who had worked the land for most of his life and despite his age still loved the ladies and a bowl of nuts with his small beer. Brian used to pop in before his shift at Casa Don Juan and have a couple of beers with Allum, sadly both Brian and Alum died a couple of years ago and they are still missed.

The Babylon bar was just a regular drinking bar, we didn't have live football or banging tunes, it was a place for people to chat and watch the world go by. In a previous life, it was an all-night bar with various weird and wonderful characters like Gina who was covered in tattoos and liked to show her 'bits' off. Most hotels can serve guests all night with drinks however this is something we didn't want to get in the habit of and the local police were cracking down on noise. Most bars in the old town close at 2 am with the later night ones closing at 4 am so there was no need for us to stay open.

One morning whilst serving behind the bar 2 guys came in, one dressed in a police uniform and the other in a suit. They told me that they were collecting for the Police retirement fund magazine and would I like to contribute, I had been warned about these guys and that this was really 'protection money' although how true this was is up for debate. So, not wanting to upset the local plod I thought why not? After all, I was new to Benidorm, and judging by the scumbags that had used the hotel as a shag pad and pimp headquarters I thought it would be a shrewd move. I handed over just short of 1,000 Euros and the older guy in the suit wished me luck with my business and he would convey my generosity to his colleagues. Whilst it could be assumed that police corruption is a terrible thing in my case it was the best grand, I had spent with all my future license inspections sailing through, I never got fined once by the local plod whilst other bars used to have regular visits and the police would find all sorts of infringements, incorrect employment contracts, issues with the sound limiters, etc.

The police in Spain generally leave you alone unless you make yourself obvious to them or decide to act like a tit and get arrested. In the few dealings I had with them I was always respectful, and I showed generosity where I could, always a free coffee, brandy, etc, and no matter what the circumstances I always thanked them. I have seen plenty of ex-pats and tourists receive the angry wrath of the local and national police and their bruises and black eyes are a testament to the fact that always be nice. One time I accidentally clipped a woman's wing mirror whilst riding my motorcycle and like all good citizens pulled over to give her my details. She wasn't happy and insisted on the Guardia Civil attending, so she made a call and we both waited for them to turn up. About 30 minutes later the distinctive green Guardia Civil police car arrived and 2 officers got out, they both looked profoundly serious and it was obvious the woman had told them what had happened and that I was a foreigner. After a brief chat with her, one of the officers came over to me and asked for my documents which I didn't have on me; in Spain, this is not a good idea and you can be carted off to the local cop shop; however, he told me that he would come and see later to check my documents and I was free to go. About 3 hours later I was having lunch with the 'Duchess' in Albir when my phone rang, and the officer asked where I was, so he could come and see me. The Duchess being there was a blessing as she was a well-known face in Albir and Altea, her late husband was a lawyer for the Spanish Government, and I had met her quite by accident and we hit it off. Shortly afterward this car pulled up and the officer, now dressed in jeans and a t-shirt got out and came over to me, I'm slightly nervous and but he smiled and asked to have a word with me in private; the Duchess gave me the nod and I knew my back was covered should I need some regal intervention. We sat down and he said that the damage to the wing mirror would be 200 Euros which seemed reasonable, he said that he could give this money to the woman, a little surprised by this but with an understanding of how things worked in Spain I handed over the money, he then went on to thank me for stopping and making sure his 'girlfriend' was okay and handed me a card with his number on should I one day need his assistance. After he left, I told the Duchess who smiled and gave me that look as to say, this is Spain and things are done differently here.

Even now I still completely respect the law of the land and never disrespect Spanish police officers. I am constantly amazed at British tourists who argue, taunt, and provoke the police thinking that they are immune from arrest or prosecution. They seem to think that the Spanish police will be like their UK equivalents, they could not be more wrong. If you act aggressively the local police will pull out a baton and whack you with it and then haul you off to the local nick, you will then be presented to a local magistrate after spending a couple of nights in jail and receive a huge fine which must be paid before you leave the country. You rarely see groups of yobs in Spain, you never see idiots in hoodies intimidating or threatening locals and for those gormless twats that think they can be big tough guys, let's see how you get on. One time whilst walking down Levante beach a young British guy who had been drinking in one of the beach bars decided to relieve himself on the promenade in front of everyone, the police were called and he tried to run but after a quick chase he was apprehended and stupidly thought assaulting one of the officers was a smart move, he was beaten several times with a baton and carted away.

Chapter 3

We had been at the hotel for a month and I had decided to move into one of the top bedrooms, this was due to several reasons but mainly down to the comings and goings at night and the lack of commitment by our night porter Juan who I also inherited when I bought the Babylon. Juan, a short tubby Spanish guy in his early 40's was likable but completely useless, his tendency to get pissed every night whilst working and then falling asleep was becoming a major issue. Unlike the UK where you can fire someone due to incompetence, in Spain, you must go through a long arduous process and pay out a lot of money, in Juan's case I was trying to do everything and anything to avoid this. I liked Juan and despite him not being able to speak a word of English and my Spanish being in the early stages he knew I wasn't happy, after all; the only responsibility he had was to sit in reception all night, help guests and turf out any undesirables. I enlisted the help of Irish Darren who had previously worked at the Babylon before I owned it and after he screamed at Juan for 10 minutes it seemed that the problem had been resolved, the next day Juan was found asleep pissed on the hotel steps. I did fire Juan this time, but he came back a couple of times in the following months to help me out, he was just one of those characters that grew on you, and his 1970's Mexican porn star look was fantastic.

Gladys like Juan spoke little English and this was becoming a real problem as we were getting more British guests staying at the hotel and using the bar. She was taking on more responsibility and whilst this eased the burden on me it also created several issues, especially at breakfast. Whilst Gladys would take the orders, I would sort out coffees and drinks behind the bar, one guy came to the bar with his plate and using that typical British term “I don’t mean to complain, but” showed me his plate. In front of me was a fried egg and 2 Weetabix, he told me that he had asked for scrambled egg on wholemeal toast; I just glared at Gladys but couldn’t help laughing. Wrong orders continued to come out of the kitchen, and they got more bizarre and Gladys’s cooking needed some serious attention. In the UK we love an English breakfast, arguable they are easy to cook, in Gladys’s case eggs were fried in olive oil which made them taste awful and looked green, she deep-fried the bacon and couldn’t grasp the fact that baked beans despite being a vegetable were part of the breakfast. Breakfast service would then be interrupted by her having a full-blown row with the new cleaner who despite her 4’6 height and slight demeanour she could give both barrels if provoked. The cleaner was the mother of a Spanish guy that worked in a bar around the corner and I took her on as a favour, she was completely useless, but I didn’t want to upset her, so she carried on being the slowest cleaner in the western world for more than a year.

Once we had got Gladys cooking breakfast properly and she started to understand the orders and things started to improve and we picked up a lot more trade, although many came in to see if she would cock up the order or witness a potential row with the cleaner which was a daily event. The more difficult customers were left to me, when I say difficult, I mean those customers who want to know where every ingredient comes from; are the sausages English? Where do the eggs come from? Is the ice from the tap? To put customers' minds at ease I would tell them that the eggs were flown in from Heathrow daily and we made the ice at night from bottled water, it is amazing what people will believe. Like many ex-pats that live and work in Spain, I was often asked if I live here, and do I like it here? I of course lied and told them that I hated it and I commuted from London daily, I even had one couple start debating if they could do the same from Leeds.

Bookings in the hotel started to improve as I registered with a couple of booking sites including Travel Republic and Hostel World, the latter being more for students and those looking for a cheap room. I never intended the Babylon to be anything, but a budget hotel, and all our marketing was in line with this; the one thing I needed to do however was warn potential guests that the Babylon was in the heart of the old town which had a highly active gay community. Many of our guests were gay and knew the Babylon from old and had stayed there for years. Unfortunately, some guests did not read the hotel description, and this caused some problems. One elderly couple who had booked a week through Travel Republic came down for breakfast one morning and afterward went upstairs and packed their bags and left the hotel, they left a note for me roughly saying "I don't expect for my wife and me to eat breakfast surrounded by homosexuals holding hands, we find this very inappropriate and I will be back on Monday at 10.00 am to collect a full refund". Now, like most bar, restaurant, and hotel owners I didn't allow people snogging or engaging in sexual acts in public areas, however, a couple of guys holding hands at the bar is hardly the lewdest thing I can think of. Incensed by this letter at its openly prejudice and derogatory tone I asked the local gays to come into the hotel on Monday at 10.00 am in a show of defiance; a couple of drag queens was added to the mix. The guy turned up and was immediately horrified by what he saw and turned on his toes and buggered off, without a refund. I was later contacted by Travel Republic after he had made a complaint and I defended my actions and asked them if they condoned homophobic behaviour? What could the poor girl say on the other end of the phone, she was mortified and happily accepted my decision.

I became very protective over Gladys, Juan, and the very small cleaner, and on one occasion I got a phone call from one of our regular ex-pat drinkers after a guest had been incredibly rude to Gladys, the poor woman had no idea what this guest was saying to her, but I was told that he called her the ‘C’ word. I turned up and a guy with 2 women was shouting at Gladys, I immediately told him to stop shouting and tell me what the problem was. He had booked a room for him and his wife but when he got to his room there was no en-suite, he demanded to be moved to a better room. I investigated his booking and showed him the paperwork which clearly stated he had booked a cheap room with a shared bathroom. He then started to shout again and like many men with ‘small man’ syndrome decided to get incredibly abusive. At this point I had had enough and told him that if he swore one more time at Gladys, I would physically throw him out and give him a slap; I turned around to his wife and said to her that her husband was an idiot and how dare he speak to Gladys like that. I told them all to get their bags and piss off immediately, he responded by telling me that he would call the police. In Spain swearing is common but if you disrespect a woman the police will come down hard on you, they love women and although the culture is still very archaic it is not advisable to threaten or shout at a woman. A few minutes later they were on the street and having a huge row after the wife and friend started screaming at 'small man' syndrome.

Most small hotel owners keep a blacklist of problem guests and after such situations like small man syndrome, we ring around to add names to that list. On this occasion, we told all the old town hotels that the wife and her friend were fine but small man syndrome was a problem, I hope he slept on a bench and got screwed up the arse royally.

One thing Ryan and I discovered very quickly was that people act very differently when they are on holiday, they certainly let all their inhibitions go. I was trying to doze off one night after a long day and I could hear this strange sound, not being able to ascertain where it was coming from, I got up and opened my door. I could then hear more clearly, and it was a faint "help, help", it was coming from one of the rooms. I went into the communal bathroom and it got louder so I opened the window onto the lightwell and could see a guy lying on a bed, I shouted, "are you okay?" he looked at me and said, "can you untie me?". I got my master key and opened his door, he was completely naked and tied to each corner of the bed; I said, "how long have you been here?" he then told me that he came back with the guy who was staying in the room and was tied up and left while the guy went out for some drinks. I untied him and he ran out the door still naked and headed for the stairs, he turned around and thanked me and then disappeared into the night. The guy who was staying in the room never came back and that then ended what was to become a typical night.

Most guests were happy to be in sunny Benidorm and experience what both the old and the new towns had to offer, however, some wanted to chill in their rooms and watch TV. One evening a woman came downstairs and said that her TV wasn't working, and could I have a look at it, I asked her what the problem was, she said she couldn't get Coronation Street. I asked her whether she watched Spanish TV when she was at home and she looked at me bemused and said "why would I watch Spanish TV in the UK…………Enough said. I have no issue with Brits wanting a little slice of blighty when they are abroad, surely a week without Corrie, EastEnders or Emmerdale is something most of us can bear.

A term that you hear people say when they are packing their cases before leaving for the airport is "just in case" and this was evident in what people brought with them. When showing guests their rooms they would start unpacking and I would be amazed by what people had stuffed in with their towels, shorts, and bikinis; everything from cans of baked beans which often ended up being heated in the kettle through to a full medical kit "just in case", you may find this hard to believe but they do have pharmacies in Spain. The British assume that all other countries have no medical infrastructure, and that the 3rd world extends to everything outside the British Isles, although one guest brought a spare leg with him in case he lost the one he was wearing; I doubt the local pharmacy carries prosthetic legs.

The 'just in case' extended also to clothes which meant 5 outfits for every day and this did not include allowing for bad weather which filled up a different case. Us Brits lead the world along with the Americans in buying complete crap for our holidays, and British women lead the pack on this one. I will give you a typical scenario whereby Dougie and Judy from Scunthorpe are out 'holiday' shopping a few weeks before they come to Benidorm and Judy is pulling Dougie around every shop in their local Arndale Centre (Why are all shopping Centres called Arndale?), Judy has now dragged Dougie into Primark where she is picking out several maxi dresses to cover her wobbly bits, you can hear her say to Dougie "This will look lovely when we are drinking a sangria watching the sun go down", Dougie nods but really doesn't give a shit. The reality is that they will both be completely shit-faced after 10 pints of John Smiths and a few Vodka Red bulls in the world-famous 'Black Chicken' and will never see the sunrise let alone set. She will have one of her hideous maxi dresses on with a plastic flower on the side of her head because it makes her look like a Señorita, she actually thinks she will blend in with the locals.

Ladies let me give you a tip. Only overweight British women wear maxi dresses, you would never see a Spanish woman clean her floors with a maxi dress let alone wear one. There is a reason for this, and it is straight forward, Spanish women are not fat because they eat a healthy diet and don't need to buy a dress that looks like a 1970's frilly curtain to cover up their ripples of fat.

Spanish women are also perplexed as to why British women feel the need to be covered in tattoos, especially the over 40's. Come the evening, you will see several Judy's bouncing along in their maxi dresses, their skin bright red from being a plonked on the beach all day and nasty cheap council estate tattoos glimmering on their fat 50-year-old arms and shoulders, for all you Judy's out there, just bear in mind the Spanish are laughing at you. As you read this, I can hear shrieks of anger and shock coming from some of you, why would you be shocked? You are a middle-aged woman with skin like the cover of the Beano wearing a dress that used to be on top of a toilet roll in the 1970s and you are as red as a lobster.

Whilst Judy is waddling down Levante Beach in her fashion faux par, who is walking with her? Dougie. Now Dougie is not letting the side down, he compliments his wife's terrible fashion sense with the all too familiar vest, long sports shorts and has an equally shocking number of tattoos; this is carried on his rotund physic which is celebrated by a huge beer belly which he pats and proudly boasts is down to the volume of beer he can consume. Whilst Dougie pounds the pavement his shaven head glimmers in the hot sun with wrinkles due to excessive skin on his crown, but to Dougie, he looks tough, really tough and he walks with his arms hanging like a Neanderthal; it looks like he has a role of carpet under each arm.

Unfortunately, there are a lot of Dougie's and Judy's in Benidorm which are a great sense of amusement for all the Spanish who joyfully take this piss out of them. This is highlighted in the winter months when temperatures in Benidorm can be pleasant but hardly blistering, but you can be assured whilst we ex-pats and the Spanish are enjoying a coffee in the setting sun with our coats and scarves on, Dougie and Judy will be sloshed at a British bar in their maxi dress and vest.

Being a nation of imperialists where everything British is best we forget that 99% of everything we pack in our suitcases was manufactured overseas, not that this occurs to most tourists who feel the need to adorn their balconies with union jack towels and flags. Thankfully, the Babylon wasn't the type of hotel that attracted flag hanging numpties, but it is a sad sight across the resort when we Brits feel the need to 'bring a little bit of blighty' with us. I understand why they bring tea bags; I also understand why we would take some of our favourite foods but why a flag or towel to show how British you are.

When we used to take the cases up to the rooms I would often chat with the guests and most married couples would have the same unpacking tradition, when I say married, I mean straight couples; gay couples are meticulous packers and unpackers. Straight couple's luggage normally consists of 2 large cases and 2 small cases, the woman has filled 3 of the cases, I am sure you can guess which ones. She will spend the next 2 hours sorting outfits, lining up shoes, taking over the bathroom with makeup, gels, false eyelashes, moisturisers, and things us guys have no idea or concept of.

Most of this crap is 'just in case' it rains, there is a typhoon, different types of sunburn, or anything else Superdrug could fool them into buying. I haven't mentioned hair products as this is a completely different conversation and I would need a whole chapter, needless to say, the hairdryer saga is something all men go through; "the plug is in the wrong place", "the mirror keeps steaming up", "my hair keeps going frizzy" etc. As for us guys, all our stuff fits into a pencil case and gets relegated to a dark corner under the sink.

The "just in case" is shadowed by the crap and strange things that guests leave behind. For you 'Pop Pickers' out there I will give you the top 5. Coming in at number 5 are beach towels which tend to be the first thing thrown out of the suitcase to make room for fags, vodka, and straw donkeys. No 4 comes in with no surprise but toiletries especially suntan creams, after sun, and those bottles that can't go through airport security and took up the whole bathroom when 'she' unpacked. Following up at No 3 is sex toys, I can imagine that the sheer embarrassment of having one of these discovered as you pass through security is motivation enough to discard them like a hot potato, many pairs of handcuffs, well-used vibrators, and multiple packs of condoms were regularly found by the cleaner. No 2 is the same all over the world, phone chargers; I could have opened a shop selling second-hand chargers and I used to give these away to new guests, how many times guest packed their cases, and forgot to look at the wall sockets. Most would never guess what No 1 is and you will be shocked, the No 1 thing left in hotel rooms is underwear: specifically, women's knickers. We found these under mattresses, stuffed down toilets, and hanging off balconies; ladies.......... surely you must want these back!

Whilst on the fairer sex, women are the messiest and by far the untidiest especially when they are sharing a room. My poor cleaning lady would despair if we had a group of women staying and she became suicidal by the end of her shift, it was the clothes scattered all over the bed and the floor along with the make-up bombsite that she would find in the bathroom especially around the sink, and the discarded or forgotten knickers were something that would make her small leathery wrinkled face turn red with anger and I could hear every Spanish swear word known to man and a few which were even new to me. When she came across the odd vibrator which had been spontaneously purchased at the sex shop around the corner, she would bring the little-used vibrator down in a bucket and just look at me and shake her head. I never will understand what she wanted me to do with this female smile charm, but I certainly wasn't going to pick it up or set a business in second-hand sex toys, what would the sex shop say? I have to say that despite being pretty savvy when it comes to all things sexual, even my eyes were opened when I bought a remote vibrator and tried it on one of my 'special friends' as Ryan would call them. Sitting in Spirit Bar chatting to Steve whilst I pressed the button and watch my 'Special Friend' squirm and squeal with ecstasy was fantastic and just at that stage when the orgasm was coming, I would take my finger off the trigger, how cruel. Poor Steve who owns Spirit could not work out what was going on and why the strange woman standing next to me was convulsing like a cocaine-loaded break-dancer.

The Babylon like most hotels in the old town was very much about people having a good time and we did our utmost to make sure our guests did. Sometimes things went a little too far and whilst I didn't judge guest's behaviour occasionally, they did things that were just plain bizarre. Small cleaning lady was doing her rounds one morning and she came downstairs with a face that can only be described as animated. She only knew a few English words but signalled to me to follow her, up the stairs I went and when we got outside room 101, she looked at me and said in a very strong Spanish accent "Inglish peoples……Krazy". Nothing in this communication surprised me, after all, I was running a hotel in Benidorm so tell me about it. I opened the door and looked into the room and even I was shocked, so much so I closed the door and look down at her and just said "fuck", had I really seen it?? She looked at me and just shook her head. I opened the door again and there it was, a fucking live, breathing, squawking chicken staring straight back at me. We allowed small dogs, we even had a guest who brought their cat with them but a chicken, a fucking chicken; this was a first for me. Having lived in and around Surrey all my life I didn't really come into contact with livestock, certainly not chickens unless they came ready packed and very dead; dealing with live poultry isn't something they give you in the 'how to run a hotel in Spain' manual.

There was only one option, I had to catch the chicken. I will at this stage give readers a wise and very sound piece of advice when encountering a live chicken in a confined space, do not, I repeat, do not try and chase a chicken around a hotel room; they are bloody fast, get very angry and tend to shit a lot when annoyed. So here I am chasing the chicken whilst small cleaning lady just stared at me and offered no assistance, the little bugger was fast and skilled in the art of eluding capture. Eventually, I hit on a brain wave, use the eiderdown to throw over uncooperative chicken which I did, and success, I had bagged him or her and carried the wriggling buddle downstairs. What to do with my wriggling captive was another matter and whilst my local drinkers looked unimpressed, I took the eiderdown into the street and let the chicken go; he/she went clucking off down the street never to be seen again.

Clean up of the room got underway with immediate effect and small cleaning lady was not impressed and she made me acutely aware of her disdain for Inglish Krazy peoples.

A few weeks had passed, and things were coming together, the rooms were filling up and the bar was doing well, the locals and guests loved Ryan and he was a natural at schmoozing. It helped that Ryan was a very good-looking guy and both chicos and chica's fancied him, this was always good for business and me insisting that he wear a pair of little red shorts just made him even more popular. Initially, he wasn't too keen on the red short's idea but when women started coming into the hotel just to see him you couldn't keep him out of those little budgie smugglers. What was lovely is that despite his young years he was completely comfortable around gay guys and his ability to chat about everything and anything made him very popular around the old town.

Chapter 4

The roof terrace was a shit hole, a painted red floor with crap everywhere and no electricity. I had already arranged for Joe, a UK electrician to come over and fit new sockets in all the bedrooms, knowing how women love to blow-dry their hair they needed additional sockets. I had also asked Joe to move the light switches from behind the headboards, why the Spanish do this is beyond me, but it is common; they also love to put sockets high above the bed near the ceiling. He was coming over with his wife Shirley and because he was retired, I suggested they make a holiday of it and I would supply beer, food, and lodgings in return. I would get Joe to install electricity on the roof as beer taps, chillers and freezers need lots of juice, so I needed a professional. I would have used a Spanish electrician but a couple of weeks prior I had a guy turn up to fix a couple of sockets and it took him 2 days, 17 cups of coffee, and 2 siestas so sticking with Joe seemed like a good idea.

Joe and Shirley turned up and he got straight to work, and he was quick, although there was a lot of head shaking and muttering; mainly at the Spanish wiring but he did an amazing job whilst Shirley drank beer and relaxed. Within a week the roof terrace was fully wired, I had bought beautiful rattan sofas and sunbeds from a Scottish guy who ran a shop down the Estrada. I had tried to buy from a couple of Spanish suppliers, but they wouldn't deliver, and I doubt my beaten-up old scooter would be up to job; Scottish guy turned up early one morning and we hoisted up the furniture using ropes and tarpaulin onto the roof terrace. The floor had been painted a nice shade of cream which made the terrace pop, I had ordered a load of palm trees and shrubs from a local nursery and finished the bar using some old solid oak doors which gave it a cabana look; this was complemented with a straw parasol which I bought from a gypsy on the side of the street. The roof looked amazing and I even inherited a lizard that lived in one of the palm trees and would pop out, say hello, and then shoot back into the palm. If you have ever seen Death in Paradise on TV, my lizard looked just like Harry.

My friends at Buying Group supplied the beer and pumps and even the Ice Man, who looked nothing like 'Iceman' from Top Gun gave me a free freezer as he wisely knew we would be doing good business up there. The poor bugger did not realize at the time we had no elevator, and his deliveries would be up 4 flights of stairs.

I knew at this stage I would need more staff and I started looking around and put the word out. There is always a shortage of work in Benidorm so when a bar is looking for staff you get inundated and as part of that you get your fair share of oddballs and weirdos, most have drink or drug problems and many can't be trusted around money. Luckily, I managed to find some wonderful people, and many stayed with me for the duration of my ownership of the Babylon. Steve and Wayne were a couple who came to Benidorm from Ibiza where they were looking to open a bar come nightclub, initially, they were going to buy the 'Wall' a closed nightclub opposite the Babylon but wisely they pulled out due to issues around the license. So, they came to work for me and Wayne being a good-looking 'muscle Mary' was perfect for the roof bar, gay guys who made up most of my trade loved him and he was an instant hit. Steve, his other half worked the bar downstairs and again good looks and charm made him popular with the locals and he was a true asset. After they left the Babylon, they have run some hugely successful bars and restaurants in Sitges and Gran Canaria, and I have to say I am immensely proud of them.

With the roof bar open and doing well we had a few issues to contend with, namely the number of stairs people had to climb to get up there. We could not install an elevator, so we had to warn those with mobility issues that the roof bar would not be very accessible and unlike the UK and its overzealous politically correct mantra, it never became a serious issue. The other issue was the heat, so we installed fans everywhere which seemed to work. Ryan worked many shifts up there preferring to be in the sun rather than being stuck in the downstairs bar with the oldies, although he managed to get most of them to come up to the roof.

One of my favourite bars, when I wasn't working, was Oliver's which is next to the Queens hotel, and one day, I saw a woman working at the Queen's terrace. I had seen her a few times and it seemed she worked ridiculous hours and boy what a grafter. I asked her to come and see me at the Babylon and the next day she popped in and she agreed to come and work for me, that was the beginning of Kai.

Kai was a 50 something hippy who had her fair share of life's traumas, her face told a story of heartache, loss, and neglect; her voice was one of a 60 fags a day smoker which was husky and slightly manly. Kai had been working 80 hours a week at the Queens and earned a pittance, was treated appallingly, and taken advantage of; she jumped at my offer and started the next day. She had her own room on the top floor, I had moved out into an apartment opposite, so it freed up a room and she was in her element. Kai was employed to help with the cleaning, work the downstairs bar, do some cooking, and just help where she was needed, she excelled straight away and after a while took on more responsibility.

When Kai was sober, she was great at her job, when she was pissed, she was a nightmare, she got things wrong and made a complete mess of guest's bookings. One night she was working the downstairs bar and a guest came back into the hotel and asked for his room key, this chap who will remain nameless but was a large bald gay gentleman who was very pissed and could hardly walk. Kai who must have downed a bottle of wine before his return gave him the room key and he staggered up to bed. About 15 minutes later a woman came into the hotel dreadfully upset after having a row with her husband and she had come back alone and wanted to go to bed, Kai gave her the room key and she went upstairs. A few minutes later there was an almighty scream, the woman came flying down the stairs crying when Kai asked what the problem was, she said there was a big fat bald man in her bed; Kai had given the guy the wrong room key. Kai rang me and I returned to the hotel, Kai was trying in vain to calm the woman in the bar, and I went upstairs and tried to wake a very pissed big bald gay man from a comatose slumber. Whilst all this was happening her husband walks into the bar and all hell breaks loose, initially, he assumed that she had brought this guy back with her and taken him to bed. As the details immerged of what had really happened, he calmed down and laughed............yes laughed. Thankfully, we had another room, so we shifted Mr and Mrs into a nicer room and moved all their stuff and left the big fat bald gay man in the bed; he was mortified in the morning, and how I never fired Kai still amazes me.

Around this time a guy came into my bar and after a while, we got chatting, he was buying the bar next to the Queens Hotel called the 'Beer Keller' and wanted a bit of advice. Bob was a gangly, bow-legged guy in his 50's and we hit it off straight away. A couple of weeks later, Bob opened his bar and renamed it Bar 66 based on the English football team's world cup win many years ago. Bob was a compulsive cleaner and was completely OCD, so much so he would clean your stool even if you just nipping to the toilet. Now, most bar owners have several things in common, friendly, hospitable, and welcoming; Bob was none of these and soon gained the reputation for being the most miserable and rude bar owner in Benidorm. People would go into his bar just to see how rude he really was, his pet hate was northerners; Bob being a born and bred cockney despised northerners. Unfortunately for Bob, instead of taking offense many northerners flocked to Bar 66 to see the rude cockney and took great delight in hearing Bob say "mate, I have no fuckin idea what you just said", this was particularly true when serving Geordies and Glaswegians whose accents are unintelligible to most people after they've had a few drinks. Bob would have many encounters with the local police after a terrace war broke out with the neighbouring Queens Hotel, their customers would use Bob's tables and quite rightly Bob wasn't happy about this and looked at ways of separating the 2 terraces, he even bought a dozen conifer trees which completely blocked the Queen's entrance; not to mention attracted every mosquito north of the Sahara.

The owner of the Queen's at that time was not happy with me, I had decided to drop my prices so I could get my empty rooms filled and this didn't sit well with her. She turned up at the Babylon and started screaming at me for trying to ruin her business, probably not helped by me nicking Kai off her. After a lot of huffing and puffing, she turned around to me and said, "if you want a war, I will give you war", in the months to come the Babylon decimated the Queen's business and the owner sold up and went back to the UK. Most hotel owners in the old town got on and we recognised that working together was the best way of improving all our businesses.

By now the roof bar was doing good business and although at times it would get a little naughty with guys getting amorous in the warm afternoon sun especially after a few drinkies, however, it was all innocent fun. The rickety old shower which I had left when I refurbished the roof was a particular favourite with our gentleman customers who enjoyed lathering up and showering their white dangly bits. With the roof now doing food we needed another pair of legs and Bob mentioned a young Romanian guy called Alin who was working in a hotel in the new town but was looking for something better. Alin was a pleasant and cheerful lad, only 22 years old but he understood bar work and was eager. I put him to work on the roof and we had now started to devise shifts as the roof bar was open from 11 am until 2 am, Alin worked alongside Wayne and Ryan until he was confident to run it alone. Alin wasn't a bad looking guy and the gays liked to take advantage of his naivety which used to drive him into a panic, he even rang me one day and pleaded with me to save him from the gays who kept pulling his shorts down. For me, this was good business, nothing wrong with him being molested a little after all women have had to put up with this shit for years. One afternoon I was serving beers to a bunch of guys who were sitting at the bar, the terrace was packed, and the sun was shining, Ryan was running around in his red shorts charming the women and Alin was mixing a mojito when all of a sudden a guy at the bar shouted "what the hell is that?", I looked at the bar top and this marble was rolling down it; we all suddenly realized after Alin picked it up it was his glass eye...........Holy shit, Alin had a glass eye!!! Sadly, Alin had lost his eye as a child and was saving up for a bigger one. The guys sitting at the bar were speechless and I'm sure this was a story that would be told many times after they returned home.

The roof bar was themed on 1980's Ibiza where I worked a season in the early '80s after running out of money during a holiday. I remember the cave bars and cool terraces in Ibiza town and wanted to mirror those happy memories, I think we pulled it off and I used to get some fantastic reviews. The music was a mixture of Café Del Mar and Head Candy which gave it that ambient vibe, sometimes a local young Spanish guy would bring a guitar and start playing traditional Spanish music which was beautiful, and everyone loved it. I even got a music teacher called 'Tony Cello' to stay during the summer holidays and play his cello which people loved, not everyone who goes to Benidorm drinks pints, watches football and fights in the streets.

By early summer I was supremely fit having carried several beer barrels and crates daily up to four flights of stairs, I even started getting a six-pack and Ryan just got fitter and better looking as his suntan deepened. We were both bronzed, fit, and shagging like it was the end of the world, well I was shagging; Ryan had a girlfriend back in the UK who was moving over to be with him. Jamie Leigh was lovely, one of those girls an old friend of mine used to say in his strong Italian accent "one you take to your parents" rather than "one you take to the woods". Ryan and Jamie Leigh had an extraordinarily strong and supportive relationship which was lovely to see based on their ages, rare in today's snowflake generation who live their lives on social media and have egos the size of football stadiums.

The two of them stayed in the first apartment we rented in the Alameda and set up home as a bona fide couple, they became regular faces around the old town and Jamie got a job working at the Guinness Bar on Levante Beach. Jamie was a great influence on Ryan, and you could see they were a happy couple, their joy was heightened with the arrival of Dooley the Cocker Spaniel which was mad but completely lovable.

Over the past few months, I had slept with and enjoyed the company of various women that I had met in the hotel or in the new town, specifically Café B the notorious meat market on the square. Bob was a bad influence, his misery at running Bar 66 was softened by the bottle of Soberano brandy he drunk most nights whilst tending his bar, the very fact that it has 'sober' in its title is a complete contradiction. Bob and I were very different, but that difference made us great mates, before coming to Spain Bob had been a union official with the RMT and worked closely with Bob Crow; being an avid socialist his politics and mine were complete opposites. I would take great pleasure in putting up the odd Margaret Thatcher photo in his bar without his knowledge and watch Bob go into a meltdown on its discovery. I would help him close up at 2 am and then we would head into the new town and get blindingly drunk from the freebies dished out by the staff at Café B, Bob had a thing for the girl who worked the top bar, so this always helped in securing free drinks, failing that we always had the Indian guy who worked the terrace bar, I had known him for years. Café B was always full of adolescent 40 - 50-year olds on hen and stag do's, most were married but took their rings off and wanted a fling before they returned to the drudgery of their real lives back in Blighty. Benidorm has always been a mecca for Brits, especially from the north where towns and cities like Salford, Manchester, and Bradford are dominant in the Benidorm mix.

For Bob and I, Café B was a playground which never stopped giving, waking up most mornings in a stranger's bed with a raving hangover was the norm; never knowing the name of the woman whom I had slept with was all part of the 'Costa' life and we were living the dream. Bob liked psychotic women who took lots of medication, an anti-depressant dependency was a real bonus; anorexia would seal the deal. He would start relationships that would be highly volatile which would normally end with him ringing me in the early hours of the morning to help him get rid of the latest nutcase. One of these highly volatile nutters who was staying at the Babylon and had recently succumbed to Bob's charms had decided in the early hours of the morning to have a row with herself in his kitchen, fuelled by booze and copious amounts of meds she was a premier league nutjob; I had to rescue Bob from this situation after he rang me at 3 am pleading with me to help him, we successfully coaxed her out of his apartment. As Bob's bar became busier and the pressure mounted, he would take on barmaids who would last a few weeks, mainly because Bob slept with them. Bob's criteria for employing a barmaid was based on looks, whether he fancied them and ideally a drug dependency, so many girls that worked for him couldn't pull a pint, speak English, and had no experience; this was all a bit tricky when you are working in an English bar. Bob ran a very successful bar but not being able to speak Spanish hindered him, many times I was called to interpret only to discover that the 6 people sitting on his terrace where Dutch and speaking better English than Bob.

This lifestyle did not help with running the Babylon and whilst Ryan was playing happy families, I was making up for the years of not going out when I was married. Gladys would give me that glare as I rocked up to the hotel and tried

to make sense of the day to come, however, Gladys was a true star and always had my back.
My biggest problem was my complete inability to drink, ever since a teenager, I have been a 3-pint wonder, I soon realized that drinking water with my beer helped my recovery a lot quicker, I also started to get up earlier and clean the roof terrace before opening. The early morning in the old town was magical and hosing down the roof, watering the plants, and putting the towels out for the day's customers was wonderful, the solitude and stillness was my favourite time of day. It also helped me focus and reduce my drinking.

Like all bars, we would have our regulars and the roof bar attracted large crowds who loved the whole ambient chilled vibe, it was a great formula that made good money. When summer came, we were in full swing and I needed more staff, and along came Johnny and Alistair. Johnny a southerner with infinite amounts of charm was tall, good looking and experienced; Alistair a Bradford lad had run his own hotel back home and moved out to Benidorm for a new life, again he was tall and good looking with a gentle and warm demeanour. We needed 2 working upstairs, one on the bar downstairs, and someone cooking food, it was becoming a big family; the rota was getting bigger and I promoted Gladys to Manager as I needed a strong leader and a Spanish speaker to deal with deliveries and the odd bureaucrat that walked in.

Many staff came and went and during the time I had the Babylon we had some very odd people working there, especially the cooks and the handymen who were transient and completely unstable. My first cook, a guy in his 40's claimed to be ex-forces and suffering from PTS and used to cry daily, he would come downstairs with a black eye or a cut lip after his wife had beaten him up, he lasted a few months and then disappeared. Of the 3 handymen I had, the first was deported back to the UK after being apprehended by Interpol, the second a Spanish guy had a row with some guy in the downstairs bar, took his shirt off, and ran down the street never to be seen again; the third, Jason was far more normal and stayed a decent amount of time and eventually moved to the hills to raise goats, grow olives or something rustic.

I even employed 2 Irish girls who were props and stood at the end of the street driving business to the roof bar, however, this ended quickly when a restaurant in a neighbouring street complained to the police and they paid me a visit, luckily due to my ongoing contribution to the Police Retirement magazine I wasn't fined, and they left after a cup of coffee and some breakfast. Alin, Johnny, Alistair was now well and truly settled, and the boys were pulling in the punters, skimpy shorts and vests certainly helped and the roof bar was becoming a regular gay fest.

Chapter 5

As Bob and I slowed down our daily jaunts into the new town and Ryan and Jamie were getting on with their lives I was getting lonely, living in a holiday resort has lots of bonuses if you are a single guy but random sex does get boring and relationships become more important. The late-night bar opposite my apartment called 7th Heaven was run by Dan and Kev, it was one of my regular haunts which although was classed as a gay bar attracted a mixture of straights and gays and was small and cosy. I used to finish at the Babylon around 6ish and go back to my apartment and fall asleep on the sofa, waking up at 1 am I would stand on my balcony looking down and Dan and Kev would turf up to open their bar, I would often be the first one in there and many times the last to leave; the occasional lock-in would happen and it would be daylight when I left the windowless bar.

This was to become one of my favourite bars in the old town and Dan and Kev would become great friends, it was just one of those bars that had a great feel, and all the bar owners and workers would descend after work and all have their favourite bar stools. Kev was famous for his 'crap' buffet which consisted of a few samosas, pork pies, and anything else that was hanging around in his fridge, always wary of the 'buffet chasers' who would turn up if word got out; some buffet chasers are well known and one couple, in particular, would arrive with Tupperware ready to offload whatever treasures were put out. Sometimes it would get a little fruity and naked guy laying on the bar whilst having shots drunk off them was not my cup of tea, but Dan and Kev knew how to run a fantastic bar which they sold a few months later.

Dan and Kev were typical of many bar owners in the old town, middle-aged with professional backgrounds who had had enough of life in the UK and just wanted a little piece of sun and happiness. When you walk around the old town you will see this in most of the bars, this is where the close community and friendship stems from, and when times are tough, they look out for each other.

Just down the street from the Babylon and 7th Heaven was ‘Diva Divo’ which was another small bar owned by Andrew and Fritz which was my early evening local. Again, a gay bar by definition but like so many bars in the old town it attracted an eclectic mix of people, it also had a large Dutch following due to Fritz. Andrew, bless him would be my sounding board and would give me advice on the various female exploits I was involved in; the bar often being one of my ‘first date’ choices. Andrew would have to kick Fritz to make sure he didn’t say anything that may bugger up my chances of getting laid.

Fritz is one of many Dutch nationals living in Benidorm and after the Brits, it is the second-largest ex-pat community and brings a wonderful flavour to the bar culture. Part of the magic of the old town is the sheer diversity of the bars and no matter what your mood you can always find a bar that suits you, for nostalgia you have Bar Rumbo which is hidden away near the Rocomar Hotel and is still has its original 1970's décor and is now run by Tony's son, also called Tony.

Divo's was a chilled and relaxing bar where you could chat and kick back, Andrew was and still is impeccably dressed and totally charming, and like Dan and Kev would become a close friend and confidant. I would sit for hours and people watch, this was always more interesting in the gay scene and gave you a perspective on tourists and how they let themselves go on holiday, it was always great to see nervous straight guys come into gay bars, who were actually straight guys looking for some cock. When I used to get 'straight' guys come into the Babylon they would order a couple of pints and eventually ask me where the best bars were in the old town, I always asked them "what are you into" so I could gauge the type of bar that would suit. Many of these guys wanted sex and you could guarantee that they would eventually end up in Peppermint, a bar not for the ladies or faint-hearted.

I have always been open-minded and how people get their kicks is down to them. When I was living back in Woking I used to go to the 'normal' bars and pubs but one day I got a call. It was a Friday night and my mate asked what I was doing for the evening, normally I would go out with my mates, but no one was around so the local pub was my destination for the evening. My mate asked me if I wanted to go to a party. Fantastic I thought and he said he would pick me up in an hour. We arrived at this huge house and the front door was open, so we went in, a lovely couple was standing in the hallway to greet us; she was in her mid-forties and he was a bit older. They looked at me and asked what I was into, well me being a bit of a dancer I said, “I love a bit of soul, maybe some 80’s”, they grinned and asked me again whilst pointing at one of the rooms where the door was slightly ajar. The penny dropped, I was at an S&M party and my mind was desperately searching for a clever answer to their question. Now many people would walk straight out the door and never come back me, not a chance. I turned around and looked them straight in the eye and said, “if there’s any spanking to be done, I’m doing it”. The floodgates opened and within 10 minutes I had a queue of eager naughty women and a couple of guys looking to be punished. Having a very firm spanking hand was a blessing and I saw many a facial grimace, plenty of howls, and lots of handprints on bums. Word of this spread to Benidorm when a couple of friends came to visit me and they let it slip to some of the locals, my spanking became a regular unofficial event at the Babylon; the freezer was always open soothing the redness of chastised cheeks.

Gay bars aren’t any different than straight bars except things are a little more open, they are certainly more friendly, and it is rare you get any trouble. Testosterone is still very much present but without the anger, bravado, or stupidity that straight guys inflict on women. Since I have lived in Benidorm, I have met more women in gay bars than in the new town, and they were far classier, not a maxi dress in sight.

Classy is not a word that is used in Benidorm very often and the majority of tourists are pretty rough, the stereotypical Brit abroad; however, the old town bucks this trend, and it is like a completely different resort. The Babylon did get its fair share of roughnecks but most of these were women, and the biggest drinkers were always Norwegian women. I used to have this one woman who stayed at the hotel and would demolish a bottle of vodka every night, washed down with several bottles of wine. She would then leave the bar and trawl the other bars for lipstick lesbians, one night she had a row with 2 guys in a nearby bar and completely knocked them out as with any troublemaker in the old town she was banned from most of the other bars.

Alcohol flows in all holiday resorts and it is freely available, British tourists have a terrible reputation when it comes to managing their alcohol consumption, and all common sense flies out the window. When I opened up in the morning, I would see guys wandering around, dazed and still hammered after an exhaustive night of beer, spirits, and shots; the times I was asked "do you know where I'm staying?" which was closely followed by "it's a tall building with a bar underneath it"; seriously!!! My reply "This is Benidorm mate, every hotel is tall, and all have bars under them", the best I could do was put them in a taxi and send them up the new town.

Sometimes I just couldn't be arsed with the Brits and if they asked me a stupid question I would just say 'Que' and pretend I couldn't speak English and then I would shout for Gladys; obviously, this confused the hell out of her, and she would just ignore them. Even more amusing was when Brits would come up to the bar and say "Doooooooo yoooooouuuuuu knowwww whereeeeee theeee Bannnkkkkk isssss', fucking idiots.

PR Matt was a permanent guest and would keep an eye on things during the nights and would be my 'tourist information' go-to man. He was a prop in the new town and a very good prop, every day he would be outside an Irish bar off Levante herding in the punters with the promise of cheap booze and Irish music; his knowledge of Benidorm was immense, and he saved me a lot of time and irritation. Matt loved the ladies and like so many guys he boasted of his male prowess, until one morning when he came downstairs, he was as white as a sheet. He told me that he was taking the day off work due to his 'condition', Matt never took a day off work. I had seen that 'condition' before when I had been out with Bob; immediately I shouted to him……... Matt "you've been with Bente", he just looked at me a nodded. Bente is a Norwegian woman who has lived in Benidorm for many years and despite her 50 odd years was incredibly fit and athletic. Should you be lucky enough, or unlucky depending on how you look at it to meet Bente and settle down for a night of passion be aware be very aware. Once your pants come off and you have committed your manhood, be prepared for an exceptionally long night. Bente is not a woman that likes a quickie, unless you are an Olympic athlete, she will drain the life force out of you and spit out your soul. It took Matt several days to get back to his chirpy self, it took me several years to stop reminding him of his 'special' night.

Relationships in Benidorm are difficult, I tried several, and most never lasted, one was with a 26-year-old which came to end as she wanted children and I had reached the age where the thought of having more kids petrified me. Most ex-pats work in bars and restaurants with most shifts being evenings so there is little time to socialize or hold down any form of a meaningful relationship. Casual sex is prolific and understandable, so is drug-taking which is everywhere in Benidorm. I had one member of staff who decided that they would sell cannabis from the staff accommodation and saw nothing wrong with smoking a joint before coming on duty. I fired her on the spot, she could not see a problem in her drug-selling claiming that there is nothing wrong with it and I was totally out of order; so much so she decided to protest with a banner outside the hotel to get her point out. Rain and the local police soon put a stop to this and like most other druggies she disappeared and became someone else's problem. Daily I would kick out some coke-sniffing, weed-smoking junkie who thought it was clever to make my toilets their personal drug selling outlet. It was common to find small bags of cocaine or weed in the bedrooms which were thrown straight down the toilet, in a country, where personal consumption is legal it was a bloody nightmare. One joker who worked in a bar around the corner who was as high as a kite decided to throw sausages through each window of the hotel at 2 am which woke a couple of guests up and obviously confused the hell out of them.

Back into singledom I did the late nights down Café B with Bob and continued to get up early to clean the terrace and open the hotel, months were flying by and it was late summer. I used to get propositioned a lot, normally by lonely women traveling on their own and looking for a release, other times I would get slightly stranger requests. Whilst serving up on the roof bar I was approached by 2 German women, both giggly and obviously pissed; the slightly more

attractive one asked if I would take her down to the sea and fuck her with a back over her head, suffocation wasn't really my thing, so I politely declined. Swingers were a common sight in the Babylon, I was once asked if I would like to shag this guy's wife whilst he watched, she was like a panting excitable dog and I did think about it for a minute but saw Matt out the corner of my eye and introduced the panting dog and her strange husband to him, Matt had learned nothing from his Bente experience duly obliged and the happy threesome retired upstairs to explore and play.
I had started to do a regular 'Tapas' tour every Tuesday and took my hotel guests around the old town for a cultural experience. Most groups were great and really got into it, other groups were a bloody nightmare and refused to embrace Spanish hospitality. I used to take them to a wonderful little tapas bar owned by Jesus and his wife called AkiMeKedo, they served wonderful wine, hot and cold tapas and the atmosphere was typically Spanish. I would ask Jesus to give us a selection of tapas and a bottle of white and red; occasionally I would have the odd idiot who would insist on a pint, failing to understand that tapas bars don't sell pints, nor do they serve chips. Like a scene out of Shirley Valentine, the guy would stick his finger in one of the tapas and say sneeringly "what's this shit" which just made me cringe, I can't believe there are people actually like this still around. When eventually they did try the tapas and actually enjoy it, they would ask me what meat it was, Jesus would have to walk away at this stage as I said "Burro" or "Perro" which would be greeted with smiles, laughter, and nods; it was only a few minutes later when they asked what that was in English and I said donkey or dog. their faces dropped and

you could see tears welling up. Poor Jesus, I am sure he was desperate to tell them the truth that they had just eaten chicken and pork, but where's the fun it that??

The Brits are unique as a nation and we like our holidays to be idiot-proof, nothing should be difficult, and it is up to Johnny foreigner to learn our language and provide us with all the essentials to make out stay a home from home. I love menus with photos on them, the words beans on toast are obviously too confusing for Dougie and Judy from Scunthorpe so a photo of beans on toast is there just to give them that reassurance. I was sitting in John and Josephs in the new town waiting for a mate of mine to finish work and I couldn't help but overhear an English woman talking to her 2 young children and husband, they were tucking into a couple of English breakfasts and the kids had chicken nuggets; she said "this Spanish food is lovely"; how sweet.

The mate I was waiting for was Steph, she owned the brothel a couple of doors down from John and Josephs and she used to supply girls to some of the hotels. Steph was a diamond, a retired hooker who had a thriving business in the new town and had gone into 'management' as her body had long given up turning tricks. With a gruff voice brought on by a 60 a day habit she was friendly and always happy, I had immense respect for her and her business acumen. Occasionally in the evenings, I would pop into her place for a beer and witness sad desperate men looking to get a discounted shag and haggling over a few Euros, the beer was enough for me.

Prostitution in Benidorm is becoming a serious issue, new strip joints with 'extras' being offered are popping up and the increase of girls on the streets is alarming, especially around the English Square where revellers will happily go around a dark corner and pay for STD's. The local council is trying to clean things up and hopefully, this will happen sooner rather than later.

Luckily in the old town, things are for more sedate and the Spanish would never allow such seediness, certainly not unless it is behind a closed door.

We were now coming into September and the roof was manic most days with lots of regulars, groups and the odd hen/stag do that managed to slip in. Normally we wouldn't allow hens or stags as they always caused problems and it killed the rest of the trade, hen parties were far worse and were always asked to leave. Alistair would come crawling in after a night out, I could always tell as his eyes were nearly closed and he had this daft look on his face which said it all. Johnny was bubbly and he like Alistair was very popular with both locals and tourists, both guys were eye candy but came with brains.

Ryan was showing signs of fatigue and I could tell he was not happy; he was missing his mates back in the UK and I knew it would be only a matter of time until he went back home. Bradley my other son was over, he had just come out of the marines and was ripped after months of training, he certainly made an impression and even nicked a woman off me who'd I had been chatting up. It was so magical to have both, my sons, with me and it was an incredibly happy time in the Babylon.

Bradley brought over a few bits from the UK which were difficult to get in Spain, this was something I was often asked by people coming over and after a while, you either don't need anything or you start accumulating things. I used to say, "bring me a Fray Bentos meat pie if you have room", my kitchen cupboards were full of them and it kept Bob and me in late-night snacks for months. Normally we would go to Café Toulouse in the old town which was open 24 hours and was a mecca for the local police, binmen, and council workers who would sit there for hours and then go do some work. The food wasn't great but you could get a beer there at 5 in the morning so we didn't care, if too pissed then it would be my apartment and we would struggle to get the lid off the Fray Bentos.

The days were going quickly, especially as the hotel was busy and I was running around sorting out deliveries, running food up to the roof, and checking in new guests. I had also met a new woman, she had an apartment opposite the hotel and every Friday she would turn up in heels and a small black suitcase, I thought she was cabin crew for one of the airlines and what a pair of legs. She was Spanish and came to Benidorm for the weekends to let her hair down and eat tapas, she initially avoided me thinking I was a tourist but soon warmed up when she knew that I owned the Babylon.

I had a couple of new staff who got into the swing of things quickly, we didn't have time to carry anyone. My first pride was coming up and I had volunteered to be on the committee with Mario and Juri from Papagayo, they had a great relationship with the local town hall and represented the old town bars and businesses. The Babylon threw the opening party on the roof which was broadcast on the local radio station and continued downstairs with Jessie Brooke, Mark Marcus, and Jack Jones singing in the street, I can still see the crowd outside the hotel with hands raised singing along to Jessie doing Queens Radio Ga Ga.

Pride in the old town used to be better when it was actually staged in the old town, the local town hall decided they would move it up to Julio Iglesias Park and hijack what was a great intimate party. This killed a lot of business for the bars, since when did pride have anything to do with town hall officials!!

The rooms were not only full we were overbooked thanks to an overzealous booking agent who just kept sending them, we were using rooms across the old town and poor Kai would be sent out to find the best rates, so we didn't lose too much money. I had also received a call from a U.K. TV production company who had run a fly on the wall television series about a hotel in Devon, the program was more about what went wrong rather than right, and it made cringe-worthy viewing. They wanted to do the same in Benidorm and the Babylon was their first choice, I did consider it for a while but then realized that many of our guests were 'different' and I wanted to spare them any blushes. TV can be good for business, the long-running 'Benidorm' TV show on ITV promoted some positives and negatives about the resort, the stars of the show used to come up to the roof bar. However, a fly on the wall show wasn't in the best interests of the Babylon and I politely declined.

Chapter 6

Things were progressing nicely with the refurbishment of the hotel. We had painted the bar downstairs which had gone from 1970's Swedish pine sauna to a nice warm cream, the rooms were looking good although I did experience a slight hiccup when trying to buy new doors, wooden flooring, and architrave. I went to a timber store in Finestrat who were happy to get together my order which came to nearly 10,000 Euros, a sizable sum which I assumed would give me a certain level of service, how wrong can one be? As I went to pay the chap behind the counter told me to come back tomorrow as he was going on his siesta, for those of you that think siestas in Spain are a quirky thing that some of the locals participate in you couldn't be more wrong. This guy was serious, there was I with a van ready to load up, I had carpenters waiting back at the hotel; this guy was telling me he needed to stuff his face and then have a catnap. There is no point in shouting, gets you nowhere, I just had to agree and smile…………...fucking lazy bastards.

It was November and fiesta season was approaching, one week in the year when the locals go completely mental and have countless parades and party until the early hours. Ryan was moving back to the UK and he had got his old job back which he was happy about, I hated the thought of him leaving and it upset me. I had brought Ryan up after divorcing his mother so we had a tight bond and we were great mates, I would miss him, but I knew he was a grown man and needed to do his own thing.

My new relationship was progressing, although dating a Spanish woman is very complicated; when you date a Spanish woman, you date the whole family, this can be a little unnerving at the start especially when you turn up for dinner and aunts, uncles, brothers, sisters, and the pet goat are all waiting to meet the strange English man.

One thing I noticed during my time in Benidorm was that Spanish women were far more sophisticated than their British counterparts; this was even more obvious when you compared the two like for like. Hair, clothes, and makeup play a huge part in how a woman looks in Spain, they spend a lot of money on all three and this is more so in the 40 plus category. Highlights and lowlights are standard, even in women in their 60s and 70s, and dressing to impress is very much the order of the day; especially in the evenings when they all go peacocking, walking up and down the promenade. I spent many an hour sipping a beer and watching countless beautiful women walk past, openly appreciating a woman's beauty in Spain is not lewd or offensive, rather it is mandatory. A confident woman knows how to carry herself and you can see it in her walk and her posture, the gentle flick of her hair, the sunglasses perched on her head, and the slow but seductive steps in a pair of heels. After an hour of peacocking, they then find a bar, sip gin and tonics, and survey all that is around them, Spanish women will study, digest, and debate other women's clothes, style, and finesse. My girlfriend was in her 50's and dressed impeccably, I rarely saw her without makeup, and she could pull off colour combinations that most women wouldn't dare to try. She, like most Spanish women was a victim to the young eastern

European women that had flooded Spain and latched onto older Spanish men, divorce rates have soared and as a result and there are a huge number of over 40's women looking for love. Spanish culture and society have also changed in the last 20 years, men have not moved on and still believe that women are there to serve them and tend to the household chores. Traditionally, businesses, property, and land were handed down from parents; the land went to the boys and the girls got very little, many girls went on to university to escape this lack of opportunity whilst the men continued to run bars, restaurants, and farms. This macho culture contributed to the divorce rate as women wanted something more meaningful, suddenly Northern European men became highly attractive mainly because they come from a culture that has seen equality for decades and values women. I am not saying that women are not valued in Spain, if anything they are adored and revered, it is just in a different way and chauvinism is very much still part of everyday life.

British women tend to have their own dress sense, you could see the dresses and tops bought just for the holiday, "this would look good in the evenings when I've got a bit of a tan", or "is this me?". Come evening time I would be standing outside the Babylon and the 'maxi dress mafia' would walk past, hair plonked on top of the head like a turd on long grass; the uniform of the British woman abroad was always predictable, Spanish women tend to wear white cotton flowing dresses that accentuate their figures.

Spanish men are born good looking, they continue to grow into good looking men; just look at the Spanish police.

However, when they hit their 40th birthday they go to bed and wake up 3 foot shorter and 3 stone heavier. It is bizarre and something you start to notice when you people watch, small dumpy men all dressed in checked short-sleeved shirts, trousers, and a pastel jumper over their shoulders. The badly dyed hair is only compounded by the ponytail that is sported to distract from the receding hairline; Spanish men are still living in the 1980s and a trip down the beach will confirm this when they don their smallest speedos.

British men on holiday are easy to spot, they hunt in packs and can be seen in the many tacky tourist bars and the British Square, a mecca for shaved heads, tattoos, and guys singing football songs. A group of guys in their 50's on holiday for a week, or on a stag party can be an intimidating experience for the Spanish and Brits hold the title for being the worst. The Babylon was stag free zone, well apart from gay stags who were charming and far more sophisticated, gin and tonics all round with Kylie in the background. In fact, they were so much fun we held several weddings on the roof and I have some great memories of the happy couple dancing into the early hours.

Straight guys, especially shaved head Dougie's from Scunthorpe with tattoos have a real issue with gay guys; the times I heard the same clichés "backs to the walls boys" it became boring. I had this heated debate one time in Café B when this group of guys realized I had a hotel in the old town, they assumed I was gay and their persona changed, once they realized I was straight it changed again. They seemed offended when I told them that most gay guys would not touch them with a barge pole, gays have impeccable taste and fat blokes in bad clothes just wouldn't float their boat. I suggested that they spend a few days in the old town, not the Babylon; learning how to dress and more importantly how to talk to women as they seemed to have no idea. These guys belong to that club where grabbing a woman's arse and telling her that you are an astronaut is the way to her heart and bed, at some stage, they must realize that this behaviour is just childish. Café B was the late-night choice for tattooed Dougie, he and his gormless mates would hunt their favourite prey, the maxi dress mafia. Lots of cheap local vodka and imitation Red Bull would give them the courage to slobber, swear, and irritate any women that were unfortunate enough to be close to them. If the woman were lucky, Dougie would take them to the British Chippie over the road for some sustenance before a night of carnal disappointment. Who said romance was dead?

Standing outside the Babylon and watching the world go by was always interesting, old Spanish couples walking hand in hand; him kissing her on the cheek and discussing where they were going for dinner was lovely. I would look up at my apartment, the days washing flapping around on the balcony and the doors open to cool the apartment down after a day of scorching heat; below Miguel, my Spanish neighbour would be standing on his balcony naked whilst watering his plants, the woman opposite screaming at him to put some clothes on. Miguel who was in his 70's wasn't in the best of shape, his wife who was 30 years his junior was out most of the time, and when she was there, they would row, loudly. Miguel was a charming man who would come into the hotel for a small beer to escape the nagging, she of course would come and find him and continue the argument that he had escaped earlier.

Calle Alicante was never without incident, when it rained a river would flow past the Babylon from the headland, and bins, mopeds and even the odd car would float past looking for a wall or shop to crash into.

I have always loved the old town, a few little cobbled streets with so much life and always buzzing. The tourist season always started in March on St Patrick's day with thousands flying into the new town and street parties were common. The old town kicked into life a couple of weeks later and after a winter of refurbishing, cleaning, and being skint the small old town bars were ready to welcome regulars and newbies.

Many bars changed hands over the winter months and new owners would bring their own spin to a bar, sometimes subtle and other times completely radical. An example of this was when Dan and Kev sold 7th Heaven it was rebranded as ‘Dolly & Trolleys’ a tranny shack which had a slightly bizarre airline cabin crew theme, it was a complete disaster especially when they charged 12 Euros for a bottle of Corona and a glass of Cava. As is often the case new bar owners come to Benidorm with no previous bar experience or an understanding of the old town market or clientele. Some of the most successful bars have always kept things simple and played cheesy music which is always a great way to get people in the party spirit.

Sensations which is owned by Marco is just up from the Babylon and is a typical example of a fantastic cool bar that has stuck to a formula of intimacy, friendliness, and fun. Sammy who has been his right-hand man behind the bar for many years compliments the whole atmosphere and I have spent many nights in there with locals like Kitty, Simon, and the many Dutch that use the bar.

I was often asked which were the best bars in the old town which was an impossible question to answer as there were so many, also there were many degrees of naughtiness. Hardcore bars like Peppermint, Eagle, Lovers, and Bears were generally women free, and depending on your sexual slant each had its own 'special' offering. Many of these bars featured dark rooms which are rooms where men have sex, the dark is the lack of light and not to be confused with the photography term. I remember popping into Peppermint one night to thank the boys for sending a big bunch of guys up to the Babylon Roof, whilst I sat there chatting, I could hear this slurping noise; I look around and one guy was noshing off another right next to me. For those that need a quick translation of noshing off.........blow job.

The language of sex, especially in the gay scene was very much evident in the many conversations I had with guests in the morning over the bar. The standard "how was your night" was often answered with a graphic description of guy meets guy, got pissed, went back to the room, and shagged. The details were far more colourful, but I think you get the picture. My vocabulary exploded with terms like rimming, blind unicorn, felching, etc which became part of my morning chat with guests.

Like all hotel and bar owners, discretion is all part of the job. Infidelity is common when people are on holiday and promiscuity within the gay community is rife. I was always very conscious not to take photos on the roof bar as when added to Facebook could be interpreted the wrong way by some unsuspecting partner. In many cases, there was no wrong interpretation, but it was not my job to 'out' bad behaviour, after all, we were a very liberal and open hotel.

Days on the Babylon roof were a mixture of great music, flowing drinks, and the occasional party. We once held a James Bond Party where there was a prize for the best Bond and Bond girl, I ended up with most of the gays coming as a Bond girl which ranged from a very convincing Ursula Andress to a very bad Halle Berry. There was a lot of bitching and sniping when the prize went to Ursula, but she deserved the 100 Euros, the fact she had hairy legs was overlooked. Other parties often descended into mini orgies, this was of great amusement and delight for the elderly woman who lived in an opposite apartment and had a weekly free show from her balcony.

One of mine and all bar owners' biggest frustrations is the constant complaints and denuncia's filed at the local police station by residents specifically in apartment blocks. Many of these residents moved in long after the bar had been there yet complained endlessly about the noise, music, and anything else that would solidify their claim. Since Spain introduced a smoking ban in bars, restaurants, etc people go outside to smoke, this creates noise especially at night, and in turn, the complaints are increased. Another tactic used predominantly by old Spanish women is to throw a bucket of water over their balcony onto unsuspecting revellers and smokers, I'm not sure how legal this is but the police seem to allow it and it has become a traditional way of 'watering' down revellers fun.

I have always wondered how many people are killed or injured annually by things falling off balconies. Coming from the U.K. where most people live in either houses or apartments that have no balconies it isn't something that I ever thought of or considered until I moved to Spain, I wonder how many cups, glasses, lighters, etc have fallen from the 17th floor and bounced off some unsuspecting poor sod walking their dog. The times I have sat having a coffee, some breakfast, and droplets of water, dust and small debris have floated down on top of me, I hate to imagine how many hairs, dried skin, and other gross things have landed in my coffee.

My apartment has a large balcony with glass balustrades which get dirty from sand and sea spray, to clean them is a major task but I don't bother, not because I'm lazy or afraid of heights, I just don't trust Spanish construction. After I witnessed the bad wiring and plumbing in the Babylon, I formed an opinion fairly quickly that Spanish builders and tradesmen spend more time thinking of their afternoon lunch and siesta than they do about the quality of their work. The other piece of evidence that supports this theory is the Spanish hate spending money, they are incredibly tight and will drive around for hours to avoid paying for parking, they will share a small coffee between 2 or 3 people and will wait an eternity for a price to drop before buying something. If this same logic is applied to buying building materials then I am justified to be worried about leaning over my balcony, not to mention the slight crumbling of the bricks and mortar which also worry me. I wonder if there is a yearly figure for bodies dropping off balconies onto people whilst they are drinking coffee.

This issue of balconies and dangers around them extended to the Babylon roof where I strategically placed plants and trees around the edge of the terrace to avoid people leaning over the edge, alcohol, and heights are not good bedfellows and the last thing I wanted was one of my customers taking the ‘quick’ way down. This however did not deter 2 drunk idiots from throwing their drinks over the terrace wall onto the street, unbeknown to them that a funeral party was walking by and several of the mourners got covered in Kopparberg mixed fruit cider. Within a few seconds, all hell broke out on the street with incredibly angry women dressed in black vying for blood and all looking up at these 2 morons. The police arrived a few minutes later and after a lot of screaming and shouting at the 2 morons it was agreed that they would go downstairs and apologies profusely to the mourners and offer any restitution that would make things better. I made them pay their bill first.

Customers on the roof were generally well behaved and there were rarely any problems apart from the odd pissed argument, which was common especially with married couples. One local who will remain nameless was famous for stripping off completely and walking around with his dangly bits in full view, this he did a few times on the roof until I told him that this would not be tolerated anymore, even the old woman opposite wasn't impressed. If he had a six-pack and looks of a Greek god then this would be considered adult entertainment, but this middle-aged gentleman had the body of a carthorse and the looks of a dog's arse.

There are 2 nudist beaches in Benidorm, they are mainly used by the gay guys who find respite from the throngs of tourists that descend on Benidorm's 2 main beaches and the smaller old town beach. For such a catholic country this might come as a big surprise, but the Spanish are incredibly liberal in their views towards sex and how it is displayed. There are several sex shops, saunas, cinemas, and 'adult entertainment' venues that serve the gay community, words like glory holes and cabins are all part of the appeal. You will find these shops and venues nestled in-between restaurants and bars across the old town.

Whilst nudity in the Babylon was confined to guests' bedrooms and the occasional impromptu display on the roof, a thin line was often drawn during pride weekend in September and Pink weekend in May. Many of my esteemed guests would join in the festivities in nothing more than a black leather thong which always raised a smile when you had a dozen big burly bears all sat at the bar with their big hairy arses plonked on little wooden bar stools. The amazing costumes worn during these 2 events always brought and still do shock, gasps, and giggles from both the locals and tourists alike.

Pride was always a big event in the old town calendar, but I always preferred Pink Weekend which was similar but on a much smaller scale. Held up on the headland it was organised by Geoff who is well known in the old town for running newspapers, clubs, and more recently a beachfront bar; he is also an accomplished DJ and has spun the discs on many an event. Working with Geoff is Sammy Kruz who as previously mentioned works in Sensations with Marco, Sammy is a fantastic presenter and really gets the crowds going. The whole event is so chilled and has dancers, live music, and lots of local flavours, there is of course booze for sale, and we all danced until the early hours in pink and white outfits.

One of the wonderful things I used to see during pride and pink was the coming together of the whole community to celebrate not just being gay or as the PC crowd calls it, LGBTQ, but complete strangers who felt part of something that was out of the norm in their daily lives. Straight guys losing their inhibitions and joining in, singing, and dancing, hugging new friends and after years of prejudice realizing that who we sleep with has no real bearing on who we are as individuals. There are of course and always will be the odd idiot whose prejudice is only blinded by their own lack of self-worth, thankfully these Neanderthals are put in their place and scurry back to the new town where they can find comfort with all the other Dougie's.

Chapter 7

When you open a hotel, you need an endless supply of patience, for those that snap easily this is not a career I would recommend. Tourists, especially the British leave their brains at home and the moment they arrive at the airport a major dose of stupidity creeps in and stays with them for the next 2 weeks. This level of stupidity increases once they get to the resort, this is the moment when you know the book of stupid questions will come out. Beneath the bar we used to keep a little blackboard with the top 5 most ridiculous questions asked by a guest, this was routinely updated, and I was constantly amazed by the incredible thickness of guests' requests or inquiries. At breakfast they would ask "where do the eggs come from", this simple question was based on the ridiculous assumption that Spanish eggs were somehow inferior to British eggs, I of course put their minds at rest and told them that they were flown in daily from Heathrow.

I might sound a little harsh when I call tourists stupid, they are, their actions defy belief, and sometimes are barmy and totally stupid. They will happily go out when they are in the U.K. for a few beers, have a kebab or Indian, and go home with a smile on their face; they pay little regard as to the cleanliness of the kitchen where their food came from, where the ingredients come from or stuffing their faces after taking a piss in a doorway. However, put them in a foreign country and all of a sudden, they become food, cookery, and environmental experts who want to know the origins of every ingredient and will always compare it to what they have in the U.K. The number of times I heard "not sure about these Spanish sausages" or "the tomato is a funny colour", the sausages were British sausages and tomatoes, well they are tomatoes.

As a budget hotel, the Babylon fitted nicely with those guests that were looking for a small personal hotel that had no frills but made up for it in quirkiness and friendliness. Many a time I would get a guest asking me where the minibar was, or they could not find the room service menu. I especially loved the complaints that come under my 'Are you fucking kidding' banner including one guest who complained that no one told her that it would be hot in August, or the other guest who didn't like the fact that everyone spoke Spanish in the shops. Most guests were wonderful, and as much as it pains me to say being a Londoner, the northerners were the friendliest and best fun of all. Northerners have a different mentality than us southerners, they seem to let things go far easier and know how to have fun even on the most miserable of days (yes it does rain sometimes in Spain). One guy from Portsmouth complained that the rain had ruined his holiday and he wanted a refund, for me the rain was both a godsend and a curse; the roof bar had to close but the hotel bar would be rammed all day and we would make a fortune.

Food as I said earlier is a contentious issue with the Brits abroad, whilst most bars and restaurants would love to showcase local specialties and dishes the reality is Brits want their English breakfasts, roast dinners, and chips with everything. We tried several times to introduce the odd fish dish, a Paella, and even tapas but each time we went back to burgers and nuggets as these sold. O'Mara's, which was opposite the Babylon, did a roaring trade in Roast dinners and meat pies and still do, Ned and Dave who own it know what the punters want and serve hearty meals every day.

Probably the most frustrating yet stupid thing guests used to do was go out in the evening and take all their money and their passport, only to discover later on that both had gone; through being drunk and losing it or being pick-pocketed. They would come down in the morning realizing their misfortune and assumed that we could get both back with a click of the finger; in reality, their day would involve ringing around relatives to send out money to the local Western Union and a trip to the consulate in Alicante where they would have to pay to have an emergency temporary passport issued. The fact that we provided safes in the rooms seemed to have missed them by and that stupidity bit had kicked in.

The most common issue that guests had was the 'trots' or 'Delhi belly' which of course they blamed on the water which is safe to drink and it is the minerals that can upset your tum tums; the fact that most guests were drinking more alcohol in a week than they normally drank in a year, of course, had nothing to do with it. The unfortunate by-product of a dodgy tummy was the shits which came like a tsunami without warning and many a guest came down in the morning very red-faced after shitting the bed. We of course charged them for a new mattress and a full deep clean which unbelievably some guests took exception too as they thought we would just change the sheets.

Guests who drink will inevitably end up in slightly precarious situations, hospitals and police stations figured highly on our weekly roster, being arrested in Spain is not something one should consider as part of their holiday; human rights haven't quite reached the Costas and the local plod will happily chuck you in jail for a few days. The most common cause for people being arrested was fighting with groups of lads kicking off in the new town as they became drunker and drunker.

As I previously mentioned, women are the untidiest guests, but a hotel owner can bring in a lot of female business if sockets, mirrors, etc are in the right place and the rooms are 'woman' friendly. Typically, most issues are around hair and makeup and as a 'hotelier' these are important things I had to adapt when I designed the room layouts. I have learned that women have a routine that cannot be altered or messed with, hotels could increase their revenues if they observed these routines, and if possible, support them through changes to rooms. Hair washing to men is a 2-minute exercise whilst in the shower, for women the correct shampoo, conditioner, and big fluffy towels are prerequisites. Then there is the natural drying off time which can last upwards of 30 minutes and normally a bottle of wine is a great way of killing that time. Hairdryers are key, a cheap nasty one bought from the local chino will not do, we ended up buying half a dozen high-powered hairdryers with pointy things on the end; you can tell my knowledge on this subject has its limitations. I even installed new sockets at floor level next to a large mirror, these sockets were located far enough away from the bathroom to avoid steam, the eternal curse of all women's hair. One issue that arose that was completely unexpected was when a hen party stayed, they were getting ready to go out and suddenly screams and yelps came from their rooms. The screams were not due to a big hairy spider, or anything sinister; the fuse had blown; I had 9 women who were all midway through drying their hair, some were straightening their hair and the others were ironing dresses. The fuse board just wasn't designed for 9 glamour pusses all getting ready at the same time. Luckily, they all improvised and got through the ordeal and went and kicked arse with their Christian Louboutin's.

The cleaner was getting better and her mood swings had been replaced by long bouts of silence until one of the guests did something bad. I was serving coffee in the bar and she appeared with that psychotic 'look what the fuckers have done' look, mumbling under her breath she ushered me up to one of the guest rooms, she was seriously angry. I could tell as she just shook her head this time, no words just a shake. As I said earlier, guests leave stuff in rooms, but these particular guests decided to leave shit all over the bed, the walls, and the floor, this was not a case of a bad tummy; this was far more sinister. In addition to the copious amounts of shit was all their possessions including passports, laptop, medication cameras, and clothes; normally I would confront a guest and make them pay but these guys just vanished, and we never saw them again. Spanish law says you must keep lost property for six months which we did I sold the items of value to cover the clean-up costs. The cleaner decided that there had to easier ways to earn a living and departed the next day.

In general, most guests were fantastic, and we had many regulars that came back several times a year, in the winter months we would have guests staying right through as it was often cheaper than staying in the U.K. and paying for heating. The nature of the old town tends to attract the more eccentric tourists in the winter, I remember this wonderful old chap called Charles (Chuck) in his 80's from Michigan in the good old USA. Every January he would come to Benidorm for 3 months, something that his wife fully supported and even encouraged, he would arrive bent over and crippled with arthritis. Chuck was a lovely friendly guy who threw himself into the local scene and I suspect the 3 months in Benidorm was for him to service his carnal desires. Chuck, like many older gay guys, had lived his whole life as a lie, married with kids and conforming to a society that offered ridicule, persecution, and of course the occasional good beating by the local rednecks. With the warm winter sun Chuck's arthritis soon subsided and what was a crippled old man in pain turned into a sprightly happy bar hopper who would spend some of his happiest days and nights in the small bars of the old town.

Not all my guests were escaping the cold of the U.K., many were escaping life, heartbreak, and other crap situations. So often I played social worker, counsellor, lawyer, and when really needed......friend. Many a tear was shed over the bar from men and women who had come out of abusive relationships, been cheated on, or just had lost their way in life. For many of them, being in Benidorm offered an escape from the realities of their situation. One young guy who must have no more than 19 checked in and it was obvious it was his first time away from his parents, he was so nervous and could hardly speak. He had a couple of beers and I could tell he was waiting for the right moment to talk to me, I asked Gladys to take over the bar and I sat next to him and asked if his room was okay and was there anything he needed; I think he just needed a friendly face and some comfort. The poor lad was terrified, he wanted to tell his family that he was gay but couldn't find the courage, how do you break it to your mother who is dreaming of grandchildren in a few years and your father who expects his son to be 'manly' and talk football, motorbikes, etc. Benidorm was a great way for him to experience the softer side of the gay scene, despite some previous comments on how naughty things are here the reality is a close-knit and caring community. I remember saying to him that gay guys can have all the things his parents want and what would matter to them is his happiness, wellbeing and that he has love in his heart for someone special, whether that be a man or a woman. It was lovely to see over the next few days this young man come to terms with his sexuality and just let his hair down and enjoy himself. I never saw him again, but I hope his parents hugged him and told him that they loved him.

The one thing you can be assured of when in the old town and especially when in the bars is a sense of belonging. Those that travel here on their own find new friends very quickly and therefore so many people come back, often just to see the bar owners and workers. For many of my guests who had visited Benidorm for the first time on their own, they just needed a little encouragement and help to find the right bar where they would feel comfortable. It used to annoy me when bar owners and their staff would ignore single guys sitting at bars, I used to make sure they were made welcome and I would introduce them to the regulars and occasionally I would pair 2 single guys together. It was a bit trickier with women as they tend to be a little more particular about who they drink with and often they don't want to attract unwanted attention. I would offer to take them to my local tapas bar and then onto Divo Diva or 7th Heaven where they would be welcomed and made to feel part of the family. Being the boss, most women felt comfortable coming out with me and there was never any ulterior motive on my part, well, maybe the hot ones got a little more attention. Again, those bars that offered that personal service gained a customer that would spend money and loyally return most days.

My personal life was getting complicated, my Spanish girlfriend had become a serious bunny boiler, she even copied my apartment keys without my knowledge, and one day when I got home there she was sitting on my sofa as bold as brass. She had no shame in telling me that she had a set of keys cut and had then moved everything around, she had also brought all her toiletries; she even had the cheek to tell me to get rid of my cat who just happened to named 'CAT'. A beautiful fluffy rescue moggy who had a tough life, she sported a broken tail, lazy tongue that hung out, bad breath, and bad eyesight. A major top tip, if you have a cat that has flees, do not under any circumstances try and bathe them; not unless you want the cat going completely nuts and clawing your face and arms. One funny thing however is the shampoo I used had a strange effect on her fur, it stuck out like one of those dandelion things that float around. The fur stayed like this for days and no matter how much she tried to lick it, it just bounced back, she also had the right hump with me and payback was when she pissed in my friend's suitcase just before she left for the airport. Anyone who knows cats will realize that cat pee does not smell for at least a couple of hours and then it really hums. Poor Sue or Fishwife as I have called for years on account of her shocking language was not amused when her case popped out on the carousel at Gatwick stinking like an old nappy. CAT meanwhile just carried on licking her vast ball of fur and glared at me with a mocking smirk. Sadly, CAT moved onto the litterbox in the sky a few weeks later.

I knew CAT would last longer than my Spanish girlfriend and she was dumped, and the locks were changed. This however didn't stop her stalking me for several months with her going into the local bars asking where I was, thankfully the bar owners all got amnesia and couldn't remember the last time they saw me.

After losing CAT and dispensing of the girlfriend I had my apartment back, I missed CAT, but I did not miss makeup, creams, shampoos, and all the things that women seem to have in their bathrooms. I even went back to hanging my washing on the balcony which she thought was common and not the done thing, the fact my pants used to hang for days was only a time-saver; why put them away when you can have an outdoor hanging wardrobe. I happily went back to leaning on my balcony at midnight waiting for Dan and Kev to open 7th Heaven.

I decided that I would take a break from dating women, I just could not be bothered with all the aggravation that went with a relationship. Over the years since my divorce, I had been out with some raving nutters who either wanted to get married after 3 months and have babies, one who used to lock me in a room, and that was when she didn't have a knife in her hand and, one who had a serious cocaine habit. The great thing about one-night stands is there is no commitment, no compromising, and no expectations; it's just sex; I was happy to get back to the simple life.

Chapter 8

Running a business in Spain is far from easy. Bureaucracy and corruption are all part of daily life and employing staff is a costly and frustrating process. Spanish employment law insists on draconian contracts which are checked routinely by the police and should you be stupid enough not to give your employee a proper contract you face huge fines, I received a 7,000 Euro fine for one such infringement when the local Social Security office did an inspection on the Babylon and discovered that one of my staff who had been employed for less than a month was without a contract. There are also rules on how you terminate staff, large redundancy payments and holiday pay is mandatory, and you can't take someone on for a couple of months, let them go, and then reemploy them when things pick up. This is why so many businesses in Spain operate on minimal staff and service is slow, there is also the social security payment for each member of staff which is paid monthly and is expensive; failure to pay means them taking it straight from your bank account without your consent.

I was fortunate that most of my staff were hard workers and loyal, however, I employed some rather unsavoury characters as well which caused several problems. People move to Spain for a better quality of life and for the majority it is a blissful and pleasant experience; however, many come to Spain to get away from their problems back in the U.K. Problems tend to follow people and whatever the issue is it is normally the cause that still dominates their lives. If you are addicted to drugs, alcohol, or gambling; don't move to Spain for a fresh start, your problems will catch up with you and like many people living on the Costas, you will become even more addicted to cheap booze, readily available cocaine, and underground gambling. Unfortunately, Benidorm is full of ex-pats with problems who eke out an existence by working occasionally and fuelling whatever habit they have by being dishonest and thieving from their employers.

My staff consisted of long-stay loyal staff and seasonal who either wanted something for 6 months or longer. At the end of 2012 Karen joined my team, she and I had worked together in the U.K. a few years ago in Poole and she decided that the daily trudge of office work wasn't for her, she was the reason I got the huge Social Security fine and despite my anger with her at the time for coming clean about how long she had been working for me I could not fault her integrity and hard work. Karen stayed right to the end and she now works in France on a campsite and is still a good friend.

I was still getting up early and cleaning the roof bar, Kai would come up not long after and would water the plants and have long and detailed conversations with them. Whilst I was used to Kai's quirkiness the old lady opposite used to watch with confusion as Kai waited for the palm tree to answer her. Kai's weekly treat was when I would give her all the small coppers which we collected in a pot and she would nip down to the local florist and buy a couple more plants, she was eventually banned as it took the florist an hour count it all. I used to have to keep Kai on a tight leash as she would have turned the roof bar into a hippy commune with joss sticks, beanbags, and buddhas. What I really loved was that Kai had turned what was an ugly disused space into a stunning oasis with plants, lanterns, and candles. People started bringing trinkets and even their own glasses which made it feel even more special, although I drew the line at hanging up women's underwear. All around the terrace grew bougainvillea which is common throughout Spain and has stunning pink leaves that glisten in the sun. We even installed fairly lights all over the plants and hung them on wires, so they looked like stars when you looked up.

Service was important to me; good service was imperative. We used to get a lot of women arrive early and take the sunbeds, we made sure they were treated like royalty, and even the wine was served in one of those fancy wine buckets packed with ice with a beautiful crisp linen towel to stop the drips, not that they needed to pour their own wine, that was our job. We had beautiful glasses and always provided a few nibbles to keep them happy, this attention to detail kept them there all day and they spend a lot of money, they also tipped well. Most of the guys preferred the sofas or just hanging at the bar and chatting, it was that sort of place; people hung out. Tips were always kept by each staff member as I never believed in sharing tips, if you are good at your job then why should you share your tips with someone who is not? I did however insist that they gave some to the kitchen. Alistair routinely earned the most tips and held the record, closely followed by Johnny; any tips that I got went to the cleaner which she was always grateful for as most people don't leave tips in rooms anymore as they hang on to their Euros for their next holiday. I am amazed when guest thinks they are being generous leaving the cleaner shampoo, after sun and beach towels as a way of saying thank you. Would you use someone else's shampoo and toiletries?

Keeping everything tight and correct was a daily process, regulations were stringent, and health and safety were important. We played great music but had to be conscious of the volume especially during siestas. This can be a real issue when most of your customers want drinks, fun, and a party atmosphere in the afternoon after a few hours on the beach. The police would routinely drive around the old town checking bar music volumes and fining those that breached the rules.

Even during pride, the 'Sound Police' would drive around in a white Ford Focus with a microphone sticking out the window looking to pounce on any bar owner who played music too loud. After we had hosted the opening party for pride, we continued to play music into the early hours and on cue, the sound police pulled up and got out of their car, thankfully due to my contribution to the retirement fund they just had a cup of coffee and left, they fined the bar around the corner instead. I just love how one's benevolence can eventually pay off.

There is an unwritten rule if you own a bar in Benidorm and the local plod pop in give them what they want and do not charge them. In most countries, this would be frowned upon but in Spain, this is the norm and I dished out many a coffee and brandy gratis.

There was and still is a pecking order in Benidorm and this is based on where you come from and your nationality. My ex-girlfriend, the one that had keys cut for my apartment was born in Madrid and took great exception to south Americans stealing Spanish jobs, a very touchy subject in Spain. There is a particular dislike against Cubans who are treated as the lowest in Spanish society and are employed as cleaners and maids in hotels. This dislike was later transferred to the Colombians who are now the dominant immigrant South Americans in the town, like the Cubans the disdain and distrust from the native Spaniards are truly awful. Gladys came from Chile, Alin from Romania and many others that worked for me were immigrants who worked hard, they were loyal, and I can't say a bad word against them, also bearing in mind that I was an immigrant as well.

One of the biggest issues new staff faced was the coffee machine, you won't see cappuccinos, lattes or frape mocha shit, nor is there much point asking for a soya milk chai latte to go....... not unless you want to be met with a blank expression and laughter. Spain is a country of 3 coffee choices: coffee with milk in a small cup, an even smaller coffee with milk in a small glass, or an expresso. All of these can also come with ice and that is about the extent of the coffee menu. All of these are made with long-life milk and have a very creamy taste and texture, for those with delicate tummies it can really churn if you have a few too many. My coffee machine was provided free by the coffee company with the proviso that I bought all my coffee beans from them. If you are a tea drinker then be ready to be disappointed with weak and tasteless tea, you will also spend your life constantly asking for milk which they heat to supernova temperatures and curdles when added to the tea. Luckily, good old-fashioned Typhoo, PG Tips, and Yorkshire tea are sold all over Benidorm for us tea-drinking Brits. For any non-Brits reading, don't ever underestimate how important tea is to us, for those that think it's just a hot drink don't forget that little spat a few hundred years ago in Boston when they threw the tea over the side of a boat. I like my tea strong and slightly stewed; the teabag must be left in for a few minutes; so, if we ever bump into each other during the day you now know.

Food choices in Spain are limited, if you like tapas then this is the place to live although quality can vary, the best tapas are always served in smaller Spanish bars rather than tourist ones. My only real moan about Spanish food is the repetition of the menus in all the restaurants. You can close your eyes and guarantee that a menu will have paella, lamb chops, escalope, fried fish, or something that combines all of them. Most restaurants offer a meal of the day, which is always a small salad, Paella, and then fried chicken with oily potatoes; a choice of coffee or ice cream is there to help rinse down the oil reserves that have built up on the back of your throat. Don't be expecting any vegetables as they are rarely served, although occasionally you will be treated to some soggy mush that resembles some type of vegetable and crept its way out of a jar and into the microwave. The Spanish openly joke about how bad British and American food is but after living here for a few years I think the joke is on them. Even when you go for dinner in the evening you see the same menus offering fish swimming in oil, meat swimming in oil, or salad covered in oil; the so-called healthy Mediterranean menu is something that disappeared years ago and has been replaced by lazy chefs offering shit food, if you want the good stuff then you have to hunt around. The Spanish flock to restaurants at 2 pm and as I have previously said most are coming off the beaches to take advantage of the cheapest meal of the day; prices normally start at 9 Euros and peak at 15 Euros. When it comes to getting something for nothing or hunting out a bargain deal the Spanish lead the world, this is not a compliment. I have seen a queue of Spaniards a mile long waiting for a free sardine during the fiestas; if it's free you will always see Spaniards there, the old ladies kicking and trampling to get to the front.

The 'all you can eat' buffet is not something you see in Benidorm very often as it would cause bankruptcy for anyone brave enough to consider opening such a gastronomic delight. The Spanish would have a small van parked outside with Tupperware containers ready to load up whilst the whole family would be piling their plates to the ceiling, this also applies to 'pay once' and help yourself soft drink dispensers that you see across the USA and parts of Northern Europe; this is heaven to all Spanish people who relish anything free or open to abuse. I have seen old Spanish women fill their handbags with rolls, croissants, and pastries in hotel restaurants, these are taken home and put in the freezer for a later date.

Spending 3 hours having lunch is all part of the day for the average Spanish family, this is of course followed by the 3-hour siesta; work is not a consideration. This lunchtime ritual is followed in most cities, towns, and villages it is only surpassed by even longer lunches at weekends. In fairness, you will rarely see a MacDonald's, Burger King, or any fast-food outlets being used by Spaniards, this convenience food is frowned upon but also mistrusted as a stain on social interaction. There are fast food outlets in Benidorm, but most customers tend to be tourists and the odd Spanish customer normally goes in for a McFlurry or a beer.

The one constant that never changes is the volume that Spanish women speak at. Restaurants become deafening with women speaking constantly all at the same time, if you close your eyes and listen you will hear chickens squawking excitedly without any gaps. The men sit in silence as they have learned over the years it is impossible to get a word in, I am surprised suicide in Spanish men is not higher. This need to constantly talk is not just limited to restaurants it is also seen on pavements and walkways where their babbling is only compounded by their need to walk 4 abreast so no one can get past. I have learned just to barge my way right through the middle of them preferably with a heavy shopping bag which always adds a bit more excitement in separating these rude irritating old hags. The younger generation of Spanish women have found a completely new way to continue this tradition, they walk holding their mobile phones in their hands talking very loudly whilst being completely oblivious to anyone walking towards them. Instead of trying to navigate around them I now just walk straight into them, 3 points for a smashed phone on the floor, 2 points if still intact; look where you are fucking going, you moron. This I have to say is prevalent with girls and young women who have that 'princess' mentality that they are there just to look beautiful and take constant pouting selfies so the world can reassure them of their ravishing, good looks.

My irritation even extends to the supermarkets where 'princess' selfie will stop dead right in front of you whilst she bores the world about hair, lips, or some crap she saw when watching the Kardashian's. Like all things in Spain, the supermarkets are slow, and service is bad, cashiers which are predominantly women talk constantly to each other, and should you be in a hurry, you are screwed. For a country that grows and exports amazing fruit and vegetables, it amazes me how little choice they have in supermarkets, and the quality is not great either. Having spent years shopping in Tesco's, Sainsbury's, and other supermarkets in the U.K. I was spoilt for choice, something supermarkets in Spain could learn from. The only thing I would say was better is the fish which is fresh and cheap, everything else is overpriced and pretty shit. Many Ex-Pats reading this would argue that you should get your fruit from the many small independent shops that only sell fruit and vegetables, this is true if you want out of date, rotten produce at rock bottom prices. These shops are full of Spaniards looking to save a few cents.

Supermarkets in Benidorm seem to be obsessed with pickled asparagus which is grown across the south of Spain. You will find over 100 varieties which all look and taste the same, it always reminds me of a very thin, slimy penis. Other items that dominate shelves in supermarkets are rice, canned tomatoes, and tinned pate. If you are looking for a tin a kidney beans.......... forget it. Bottled water is a staple on any shopping list along with wet wipes for your arse which after several weeks living in Spain is an essential part of personal hygiene due to the sore red rash around your arsehole due to the daily intake of grease.

If you are not frustrated with poor service, bureaucracy, and the constant drone of babbling women then some of the regulations and laws in Spain will frustrate you. Apparently, it is illegal to wash your car on a public road in Benidorm, do not ask me why but in a country where your car is permanently covered in dust and sand it seems ridiculous. If you are a DIY enthusiast or have some work to do on your apartment, do not even think about picking up a drill, hammer, or making any noise during siestas, those tools can also stay in the box on a Sunday and any other bank holiday. You could apply for a permit from the town hall which allows you to work within these restricted hours however be prepared for a long wait and even then, there is no guarantee. I now see why buildings are so badly maintained in Spain.

Should you decide to nip down to the beach and cast a fishing rod into the sea so you can catch your supper, make sure you get a permit from the town hall, but you are more than welcome to go hunting in the countryside or watch bulls being tortured and stabbed in your local bull ring. If you own a bar with a terrace and put an extra table out then you will be visited by the police and given a hefty fine, however, this tends to only apply to foreign-owned bars; the Spanish can do what they like. I congratulate Spain on leading the world in double standards and hypocrisy.

Chapter 9

What used to amaze me is the generosity of those that live, work, and call Benidorm home. The Brits are a compassionate bunch and when called upon they will rally around a cause and give both money and support, often this charity is given by those that have very little themselves. A dear friend of mine called Colin who is better known in the new town as Coco Channel, a very successful drag queen runs an animal shelter in Murcia and has saved many horses, donkeys, dogs, cats, and even some alpaca. The police and other officials regularly turn up with a varied assortment of lost, abused, or just unloved animals looking for salvation. Like Noah, he brings them in and finds a shaded tree, enclosure, or a corner somewhere to home them, unlike Noah they do not come in one by one rather a dozen donkeys and some peacocks all at the same time. Colin relies on the generosity of the Benidorm ex-pats who regularly host events and have collection boxes in their bars, thanks to the generosity of these ex-pats and Colin's tireless work many animals have been saved and rehomed.

What many people don't realize is that Spain has a major issue with abandoned dogs and cats which if not rehomed or claimed within 3 months go to killing stations, this sadly is compounded by the many Brits who move to Spain and then change their minds and move back to the U.K. minus their new pet. These dogs and cats are just left to die and are found roaming streets in most towns and villages, things have become so bad that locals are now putting down poison to kill off these animals not because they are stray more so because they are breeding.

I was sitting at a bar in the new town next to the yellow brick road, this is the name of a grassy strip that runs from the top of the town right down to the beach. The yellow brick road is well known for gangs of cats who can get quite vicious when they're hungry and sit there with a napkin under their furry chin licking their lips waiting for a frail old human to trip and fall.........dinner time. Whilst they were sitting waiting for their next victim a small white van pulled up with the local council logo on, two guys got out and grabbed some huge poles with nets on the end, similar to those used to catch butterflies. I knew there and then that they were the cat killers sent out to catch a few moggies, some would argue that this is a vile profession, but I can understand why this must be done. The two guys trotted off into the yellow brick road armed with their nets looking for their furry prey, within a few seconds every single cat legged it and these two clowns stood there scratching their heads. I can see many furry paws showing the finger to these 2 murdering morons.

Whilst the spread of abandoned dogs continues in Spain at an alarming rate, dog ownership amongst the Spanish is extremely high. Most live in apartments so most of these dogs are small and yappy. My sleep was routinely disturbed by a chorus of chihuahua's, poodles, and rat-like mutts all barking at each other from their respective balconies. By 9.00 am the old town cobbles were awash with these yappy fuckers pissing everywhere and squeezing out chipolata size shits ready for their owners to bag and take away.

Thankfully, owners are now expected to carry around a little bottle of soapy water to wash away their woofy piss trails.

One huge frustration felt by bar and restaurant owners but something that is completely oblivious to the Spanish is when dogs piss up signs, barrels, and stools. Such is the cheek of dog owners allowing their pooches to piss anywhere that bar owners have now started to throw buckets of water over the offending dogs and in some cases the owners. Many would think that living in a resort with miles of sandy beaches would be a wonderful playground for dogs, however, dogs aren't allowed on the beaches and must do their business on pavements, and those few green spaces dotted around the town. There is even a new trend where dogs are now being pushed around in baby strollers, although these strollers are specially designed for dogs and cost a fortune. Just when you are about to lean over and look at a sweet baby burbling in a stroller you are greeted with a furry rat type dog, some even are wearing sunglasses.

Open spaces in Benidorm including the promenades are used heavily by joggers and speed walkers which I am one of. Most mornings I wake up early and join the many Spanish all looking to keep trim and keep good health, albeit they smoke like chimneys and stuff their faces daily. There is an unwritten rule in most countries whereby people walk either on the left or the right of the pavement allowing for smooth traffic flow, the Spanish have no concept of this, and I regularly bang into both walkers and joggers who refuse to follow a simple code of courtesy, why should I always be the one to get out the way. Bob and I even considered inventing a computer game whereby the player would navigate various obstacles namely Spanish pedestrians and you would win points for everyone you knocked over, special bonus prizes would be on offer for taking out several pedestrians with a shopping trolley. I think the game would have sold well, but I think the Spanish Government would have deported me as they probably frown upon computer games that slaughter old angry Spanish women.

This general lack of consideration and politeness is not just confined to pavements, the beach is another battleground where the Spanish ignore all rules. After dragging all their crap down to the beach and setting up as close to the sea as possible, they then form a long and continuous line of parasols which makes it impossible for anyone to get to the sea. Bob and I once fell asleep on the beach, I was woken by the sound of raised voices; Bob was screaming at a big Spanish family who had circled us we were trapped. Bob grabbed their parasol and threw it into the sea, they got the message. I have seen many a sunbed, parasol, and other things thrown into the sea mainly by disgruntled tourists who find this behaviour incredibly rude.

Bad behaviour is not just confined to the Spanish, British tourists are incredibly lazy when it comes to taking their rubbish away; bottles, cans, and fag butts are left without any thought to the poor sod that has to clean up after them. One might ask how we know they are British tourists; they are easy to spot; always overweight, bright red, and covered in tattoos. The other small identifiers include awful swim shorts and bikinis, loud and boisterous behaviour and they always have bad posture. The Spanish women are as elegant on the beach as they are off, Spanish men either wear good quality swim shorts or the complete opposite and prance around in tight budgie smugglers. When the Brits come off the beach, they forget all sense of decorum or good taste and will happily sit in a bar or restaurant shirtless, something the Spanish would never do. The need for British-owned bars that sell British beer, British food, and televise British football is all part of the Spanish holiday experience, needless to say, this creates little pockets of bars all flying the Union Jack which I find completely disrespectful to the Spanish. I always find it amusing when you see a sign on a British-owned bar say "Bill and Brenda from Doncaster welcome you" as if this is a badge of honour; having been to Doncaster a couple of times I doubt I would advertise the fact.

The bars in the old town are thankfully far more discreet and blend in with the Spanish bars and restaurants, no flags or obvious British livery hangs from the frontage; just the odd rainbow flag to show that it is a gay bar. I have always found the bars in the old town a lot more sophisticated and inclusive than those in the new town, normally owner-operated you always get a far friendlier welcome and they will remember you. These little bars which many previously were stables for horses and donkeys were my local haunts and all within a 2-minute walk along the cobbled streets. My apartment was right in the heart of the old town so popping out for a beer was always a matter of which bar. Living in the old town also had its drawbacks, mainly noise, when the bars closed at 4 am with pissed tourists screaming and talking right underneath my balcony. The proximity of apartments was also a problem with some streets so narrow you could watch the TV in the apartment opposite. When Bob told me, he had a new apartment in Rat Alley I was surprised as this is where all the tapas bars put their bins out at night, however, Bob got this apartment for a good price, so he was happy. After a few days he realized why this apartment was so cheap, opposite lived a big fat guy who would routinely wank himself senseless on his sofa right in front of Bob.

Balconies are a window to the world in Spain and it is where you have your breakfast, hang out your washing, store your bicycle, and spy on the world. I have spent many hours watching people in the streets, sober and drunk; I do not think people realize how many nosey balcony watchers are spying on them at any one time. For many Brits who move to Spain the whole concept of living in an apartment is new to them, most have come from houses with gardens, and privacy is taken for granted. Throughout my childhood and well into my twenties most houses in the U.K. had net curtains which kept out prying eyes and you felt secure in the fact that nosey neighbours could never see whatever you were up to. Come the evening, thick curtains would be pulled to provide a double layer of security. In fact, the British lead the world on quirky when it comes to our privacy and personal space; our need to be isolated from the outside world was never obvious until I moved to Spain. When we are in our homes especially in the evenings any interruption to our dinner or watching our favourite soap is met with disdain and curiosity. I remember as a child our telephone would be sited in the hall on a little round table, off-limits to me and my sister and only used in exceptional circumstances. If it rang during the evening both my parents would look at each other and my mother would say "I wonder who that could be?" and wait a couple of seconds before answering it with her very posh telephone voice before reverting to her normal voice when she realized it was her friend Barbara. There was also an assumption that if someone rang after 8 pm it must be serious or someone in the family had died, there was no concept of just picking up the phone and having a chat with someone. I still ridicule my mother now for her telephone voice and how she used to answer every call with "Ewell 8572" which seemed to be the norm in those days.

The formality that surrounded everyday life in the 1970s was stifling by today's standards; everything was regimented, and everything had its place or time. Dinners were served at 6 pm on the dot, correct table manners were observed, and one would ask to leave the table, you also ate what was put in front of you. Dinner was followed by tinned fruit with evaporated milk, my personal favourite was the fruit cocktail, I never liked tinned pears and the peaches were awful. We always had a glass of milk with dinner which lacked the cream as the birds had pecked through the foil top and drank it all just after the milkman had delivered it.

Even our holidays had formality, most years we travelled abroad to either Spain or Greece and my father had this typical British attitude that we were superior, and we were bringing some culture to Johnny foreigner. Smart trousers, blazers, and ties were the standard attire for dinner in the hotel and formal dining was expected, what the Spaniard and Greeks must have thought of the British in those days. Nowadays all this has gone, and meals are enjoyable experiences with laughter and people are far more relaxed, I tend to avoid any restaurant where I must wear a tie or anything formal.

When I eat in local restaurants in Benidorm it is always with great friends and thankfully, I know most of the owners and workers, so the experience is always warm and friendly. Andrew who used to own Divo Diva now works in Ian's, which is a lovely restaurant near the headland, his years of experience in running a bar and his warm character really give him the skills to make you feel at home. This is typical of many of the bar owners and workers in Benidorm, many have come from highly successful careers which are ideal when you are serving the public, they genuinely enjoy serving customers and revel in stories of their previous life. The old town is a gay mecca that attracts many ex-pats who have come from creative industries including fashion, theatre, hairdressing, and photography. I am always amazed at some of the amazing careers people have had and the people they have met, one guy told me that he used to cut Princess Stephanie of Monaco's hair along with various film stars. Another was a fashion photographer who worked on some of the world's biggest magazines and shot some of the world's most beautiful women. In fact, another friend of mine used to shoot the Pirelli calendar which adorned many garage workshops and pubescent boy's bedroom walls. When he packed it in, we were all shocked and could not understand why you would swap exotic locations, 5-star hotels, and beautiful women to take wedding photos and dribbling babies. He just got sick of 5 am starts, moody arrogant models, and spending days on beaches setting up photoshoots.........are you fucking serious!!!!

The reasons people move to Benidorm vary but most are looking for a new life, a better life or they are escaping life. For many, they have reached a peak in their careers and they have nothing else to give, as you get older ambition and careers become less important and a more holistic and spiritual element creeps into your life. For me, my focus was more on the quality of life which didn't include being stuck in an office every day and treading the hamster wheel of U.K. PLC. Waking up to warm sunshine with the sound of waves is the most marvellous thing, then having breakfast in a pavement café whilst watching the world go past isn't something I ever did in the U.K.

Having my morning coffee in the Babylon was always a pleasure which more than often was taken on the roof after I had cleaned it. We used to open the roof bar around 11 am but during the busy months, we would open earlier as guests like to take breakfast up there and it freed up space downstairs. By the end of the season we had ironed out all the gremlins and the roof operated very efficiently, it had become the most profitable part of the hotel and had a good reputation around Benidorm with people coming from the new town to taste a little piece of heaven.

It was November and the fiestas were on which is a big deal in Benidorm. For a week there are various parades through the streets and everywhere is decorated with ornate and beautiful banners, garlands, and various flags. One of the downsides is the constant noise especially if you live in the old town. The Spanish will rent a bar for a week and convert it into a Penya which is a private club where they will party every night until the early hours, these are dotted all around the old town and it is very lucrative for the bar owners, not so good for us poor sods who are trying to sleep off a busy night. Following the Fiestas, the new town holds what has become Europe's biggest fancy dress party and the party goes on for several days, dressing outrageously is the norm and you will see large groups all in the same costumes all trying to outdo each other. If this is not your bag, then how about the annual 'Elvis in Benidorm' event which is one of my favourites with Elvis wannabes and lookalikes descending on the town in April. I loved going to see the bad Elvis's, truly terrible renditions of blue suede shoes sung by a Lithuanian fat bald guy dressed in that old Elvis favourite, the white sequined jumpsuit.

The one thing that is guaranteed in Benidorm is that there is always a live act on, and Benidorm boasts more live music, comedy and some would say perverted shows than any other holiday resort in the world. Tribute acts rule the stage and attract big audiences with many performing every night in several venues. For those with a love of the slightly naughty then many will remember Sticky Vicky who was Benidorm's No 1 act for many years and was famous for pulling various objects out of her vagina, something that is not recommended at home. Over the years other acts have tried to emulate Vicky but all have failed, and I would say that most were just creepy live sex shows watched by creepy old men looking to get a kick. Vicky retired a few years ago but many people still ask where they can see her, often she is the first thing they want to see. I would have loved to have been around when she was making her career choices at school and hit upon the novel idea of shoving half a kitchen up her chuff and then pulling it out whilst the audience cheered, in a deeply religious country this must have caused a few rosery beads to be dropped.

Chapter 10

On March 30th, 2013 I received the phone call that no parent wants to or should ever receive. My beautiful son Ryan had been killed and at that moment my world fell apart. As I write these words my eyes are filled with tears, the pain and desperation of a broken heart still make talking about Ryan very difficult, words can never really express what I felt then and what I still feel now. Please forgive me if I don't say anything more about Ryan's death, it is just too painful.

The months that followed were a blur, I know I drank a lot, and my good friends used to take me home and put me to bed, they would come back in the morning and get me up. I will forever be indebted to these beautiful people whose compassion and support got me through the most devastating moment of my life.

Gladys had to take on the day to day running of the hotel as I was no good to anyone, however, I realized that I needed to get back to work; I couldn't carry on drinking as my alcohol tolerance has always been low, so the hangovers and constant late nights were taking their toll. I could never be an alcoholic; I sympathise with those that are; I never realized how bad such infliction is and the impact it can have on family, friends, and those that care about you. It took time for me to get my shit together and as harsh as it sounds, I have always been pragmatic, so I never went through the stages of bereavement, I just accepted Ryan's death with all the pain bottled up deep inside me. In some ways, pragmatism can be a strong tool for coping with life and all that it throws at you. I have always dusted myself down and got back up; there is no point in stressing about the things that you can't control, only those things you can. Pain is relative and if you let it out occasionally it is manageable, for me I wept in dark corners, in bed, and away from people.

The Babylon was having some major issues with the electrics, plumbing, and sewage. Like most businesses in Spain, I owned the lease which meant the landlord was responsible for maintaining the building. Most business owners will tell you that landlords in Spain are greedy, lazy, and fail miserably to service their investments. My landlord fitted into this category, she and her brother were happy to take the rent every month and I would get a phone call if it were a day late, but, when I asked them to fix something I was met with silence. The electrical wiring in the building was completely unfit for purpose and needed replacing, the plumbing was old, and leaks were springing out walls, pillars, and coming through ceilings; one morning half the downstairs ceiling collapsed, and thankfully no one was hurt. Underneath the building was a large sewage tank which held thousands of gallons of waste, this had to be pumped out every month, the sewage system in the old town wasn't designed for the modern tourist age. This tank would occasionally get blocked and sewage crept up through the floors of the bar, not something you want when you're having your breakfast. These problems continued throughout the summer and I sent several letters and emails to the landlord, but nothing was done and eventually, I had to close off bedrooms as they were becoming dangerous and unsafe.

For many people, the pain of losing a child and all the problems with the hotel would have tipped them over the edge, thankfully good friends, amazing staff, and great customers made those few months bearable. To add to the daily issue of closed rooms and leaks I had a problem with overbookings. We used a couple of major booking agents and between me not being focused and the agents not answering emails regarding over bookings I had Kai running around the old town trying to find rooms to put guests in. Normally this wouldn't be a problem, but the old town and Benidorm had been going through a resurgence and most hotels were full throughout the year, thankfully we always found somewhere, and most guests were happy. One hotel which we used a lot was Casa Don Juan just around the corner from the Babylon and now owned by the lovely Richard, this small quaint hotel is very friendly and a fantastic place to stay and I would recommend anyone coming to the old town for the first time to pop in and say hello.

The one thing that one can't argue with is the charm and character that the old town has, despite many of the original buildings being pulled down and new apartments replacing them. This can't be said for the new town where concrete towers provide the backdrop for what is now a famous skyline. When Benidorm first discovered the benefits of tourism it was then just a small town with a few hotels and men still fixed their fishing nets on the beaches, this was the 1960's and the town had no idea that in a few years it would define mass tourism for decades to come. Some of the hotels that they built 50 years ago are still standing and are fairly attractive buildings, this can't be said for the shit they built in subsequent years, one can only describe them as concrete Lego monstrosities that were designed by a blind architect with no concept of style. I wonder sometimes if there was a secret competition to see who could design the ugliest building and then get the worst builders to construct it. What you now have is a mixture of badly built, badly maintained tower blocks that resemble a soviet council estate from the 1970s. Thankfully, they are now putting up some prettier buildings which actually look like a professional designed them, however, all of these are down Poniente where the money is, Levante still remains neglected and forgotten. One building that has gone up in recent years is the InTempo building which was at one stage the tallest apartment block in Europe, sadly this accolade was lost to other cities who built prettier and taller buildings. The InTempo tower unbelievably won a design award, god knows what for as like most other buildings in Benidorm it is ugly and out of date. It has been delayed by 12 years and when it is completed the gold façade will shine like a polished turd in the sun. However, to be fair to its future inhabitants they will be living in one of the tallest buildings in Europe with incredible views.

I prefer Poniente, it is quieter and has a much classier feel with most apartments owned by wealthy Madrilenians, that's people from Madrid to you and me. Most come here in August, the rest of the year the apartments lay empty, however, in recent years more people are moving onto the beach as permanent residents and the bars and restaurants are a lot busier. If you walk right to the end of Poniente beach you will find the Delfin Hotel and various cool and sophisticated bars which are the complete opposite of the new town. My favourite is the Deluxe Beach Bar, which is a lovely, chilled bar owned by a wonderful Spanish couple, the husband plays some really cheesy music and I have spent many an afternoon listening to Boney M and Modern Talking whilst getting sloshed on cold beer served in frozen glasses.

Music has always been an important part of any bar's arsenal for pulling the punters in and the Babylon was no different, we had specific playlists for different occasions and more importantly different age groups. I used to get really frustrated when I would go up the roof bar and we would have a group of 20 women all aged over 50 and whoever was working had decided to play their playlist which was normally the latest chart music or some crap that no one had ever heard of. The moment the music was changed the atmosphere changed with my ladies dancing and of course, buying more drinks, sometimes you can’t beat a bit of ABBA, The Nolans, and Kelly Marie to bring out the party animal. I moan constantly in bars when the DJ or staff play what they want you to hear rather than what the customer actually wants, in the Babylon, this became a sackable offense I took very seriously. The party music was always great for those long sunny afternoons when people had come off the beach and wanted to get drunk and have fun, other times we would play Café del Mar and other ambient music which reminded me of my times in Ibiza many years ago.

When I was 18, I went on my first lads' holiday to Ibiza, 7 of us crammed into a 1-bedroom apartment in Playa d'en Bossa. It was April 1983 and the hippies still ruled the golden isle, we were young, not so innocent but ready for the most amazing week. I was working for an insurance company at the time selling door to door and collecting premiums every week from little old ladies who had been paying the same 90 pence for 30 years, it was a shit job and I hated it. When I asked for the week off and they refused I told them where they could stick their job, the very next day I was on my way to Ibiza. Within 24 hours of arriving, we had crammed ourselves into the ridiculously small apartment, I and another guy were sleeping on the balcony on a lilo, the others were dotted around in the bedroom and lounge floor. The following evening there was a loud bang, it was the local police who were clamping down on over-occupancy in holiday apartments. As the police entered the apartment, I jumped over the balcony into next door which was being rented by 2 pretty Irish girls who thankfully welcomed me with that world-famous emerald isle charm. Being a very fit, blonde-haired guy who thankfully had no problems with the opposite sex the girls let me crash in their apartment for a couple of nights. Whilst I was being entertained by my new friends my mates were carted off to the local police station and didn't return until the following day a few pesetas lighter and all looking for somewhere to stay. Like all lads of that age, I burned all my money within 24 hours and needed cash quickly, in those days there was no Western Union, ATM's were scarce, not that I had any money in the bank, and asking my mum to wire me some money would have taken days. The only solution was to get a job and I had found the perfect place called the Monkey bar; this had been a firm favourite from day 1. This bar as the title suggests had monkeys everywhere, live monkeys, and they would sit on your shoulders, jump all over the bar and make a complete nuisance of themselves but they were adorable. Add a few parrots, a couple of lizards, and countless stray cats it was a zoo serving booze. I had struck up a friendship with the owner and he suggested that I work for him, not in the bar but selling beach parties which they held twice a week, beach parties were in their infancy in the early '80s and they were all about excesses.

Within 24 hours I had sold out and with my accommodation now being a glorified broom cupboard behind the bar, I would stay the season. During the day I would sell and host beach parties and in the evenings I would join up with my mates and we would party until the early hours drinking cheap booze, now I was a local worker the bars gave me a discount if I bought my mates in. One of the guys, his name was 'Vern' was still a virgin when we came to Ibiza, at 19 years old this was a serious issue and something we constantly reminded him of daily. Every evening we would hunt out any woman that might take away Vern's virginity, it became our mission. One night we were in a disco and we had all pulled, even Vern who found some Dutch courage after drinking a whole bottle of Vodka. As we left the disco, we noticed that Vern was snogging his bird by the door and then all of a sudden we could hear shouting, we ran over to see this girl flat on the floor; Vern had punched her. As we helped the girl to her feet, we confronted Vern and after some coaxing, he said rather shakingly that when he stroked her thigh his hand went up a bit further and, in his words, "it didn't feel right", what he meant was the girl was actually a 'cock in a frock' and he had just punched a geezer. So, Vern's only opportunity for losing his virginity that night was scuppered by a block wearing a frock. The next day Vern got so drunk he fell asleep on the beach and burned his balls so badly they swelled up like tennis balls. If you remember the early 80's, guys used to wear skimpy running shorts on the beach, these are not advisable when spread-eagled, drunk, and sleeping in the hot sun. We took Vern back to his apartment where he collapsed on the sofa and we put an ice pack over his expanding ball sack, a bottle of local brandy helped him fall into a deep sleep, and being the kind, considerate friends that we were we shaved his eyebrows, pubes and sprayed squirty cream around his stomach to look like he had come after a good wank. Just to add a little sparkle to the day's events we used up all the polaroid film taking photos of his balls and stomach and then took these photos around to all the bars to show our handy work. Vern didn't speak to me for over 30 years, the last time I saw him in Guildford we never mentioned Pube Gate and pretended it never happened.

The next few months were some of the happiest I had ever experienced; the whole island was hedonistic and completely laid-back, attitudes around sex, drugs, and alcohol were something that opened my eyes and I loved every second of it. Ibiza had given me a new direction; it had also shown me that I didn't have to conform to society's expectations and with a little hard work I could have a perfect life. After a month of living in the broom cupboard I was getting frustrated with the lack of space and privacy, sleeping next to crates of beer and the odd cockroach wasn't really doing for me, however, it was exciting so I never complained and Jose the owner couldn't have more kind. My luck however changed when a group of Icelandic fishermen who were on a 3-month holiday came into the bar. In those days there weren't many options if you lived in Iceland and wanted a holiday in the Mediterranean, Ibiza was one of only 3 choices and these guys who spent winters on trawlers wanted sun, sea, vodka, and sex........lots of sex. After spending a few nights hitting the bars and discos they were sat in the Monkey Bar and we got talking, they asked me if I could help them meet English women. I wasn't too keen on being an unpaid pimp so rejected their request but wished them luck, they then sweetened the deal by offering me a villa, yes a villa for the next 2 and half months as one of their mates had to fly back to Iceland after his sister had fallen off a horse and broken something serious. This villa would be mine and would be fully stocked with food and booze every week, how could I say no?

These guys earned a fortune whilst out in the North Sea, they came to Ibiza with thousands, millions of pesetas, and lived like kings, all they wanted was to get laid and go home with memories of vodka filled orgies......how I could not help them, poor lads. I moved out of the broom cupboard into a very swanky villa and within a few hours I had made these guys buy a new wardrobe, 1980's Icelandic clothes were Captain Birdseye without the coat. My early days of pimping were, of course, a great success, and my fishy friends got laid, some got robbed and all got completely fucked on that funny white powder.

I worked the whole season and made some amazing friends and met some very strange and eccentric people, the hippies in their mountain retreats were so cool and their philosophy on life is something we could all learn from. Unfortunate Ibiza moved on and the dance scene took over and turned what was once a relatively innocent island into something a little more sordid. I used to pay virtually nothing for a coffee, water, or beer now you will pay over 10 Euros for a warm bottle of water in a club.

Benidorm strangely has hardly changed since I first came here over 35 years ago. Of course, there are a lot more buildings, hotels, and bars but the essence is still very much the same. It has always prided itself on offering value holidays and used to appeal to Northerners who flocked here in their tens of thousands every year, in the last few years there are more southerners as they desert places like Marbella which are overpriced and pretentious. Benidorm could never be accused of being anything but honest and down to earth, there are no airs or graces here, simply good honest people enjoying themselves and spending hard-earned money. It does have a reputation for being rowdy with stags and hens going mental in the new town, this is true, and they tend to descend in April and May just before the wedding season kicks off in the U.K., however, they bring in huge amounts of money and whilst the Spanish moan about them it pays for their homes, cars and kids' education.

Every day in March and April there would be planeloads of stags and hens all wearing ridiculous t-shirts with some offensive, crude message on them, some crap nickname, and a picture of a cock; the women would accessorize theirs with tiaras, feather boas, or huge inflatable cocks. I am sure when they sat down at their local pub in Scunthorpe, they thought it was hilarious, let me tell you, both the ex-pats and Spanish think you are just fucking idiots. For us it just says, ‘overcharge me’, rob me blind’ because I’m a fucking stupid fat twat. When they all got to the new town, they were actually shocked when they saw 50 other stag and hen parties all wearing similar t-shirts.

Chapter 11

The summer of 2013 went slowly and whilst I bottled up all my feelings and buried the pain of Ryan's death, I still had a business to run; I also had another son who was grieving and needed a father. The building still had the same problems but luckily, we had managed to use a wonderful little pension around the corner owned by John. The rooms were beautiful, and it really had that traditional Spanish feel, our guests loved it and John was a wonderful host. The roof bar was packed most days and breakfasts were our crazy time with people waiting outside for a table. I always said that by offering our customers a fair meal for a fair price they would always come back, and boy they came back in their droves. We charged 3.99 for a small breakfast and 4.99 for a large and this included tea or coffee and toast. Like everywhere else we had the odd awkward customer, others were fussy, but most were great.

Most people just asked for a small or large breakfast, simple, and if you don't like something then leave it. It always confused me when a customer would say "no, I don't want a full English, I will have eggs, bacon, sausage, beans, mushrooms and toast": in other words, a full English minus the black pudding. Occasionally, I would go to other cafes to compare our breakfast with theirs, I must admit that ours was the best and the cheapest. I get really frustrated if you want to swap say the bacon for sausage and they charge you extra, seriously! The other thing which I have never understood is why does breakfast finish at 11.00 am? In a hotel, yes, this is because most hotels know that guests will not make it downstairs by 10.00 am so more profit. But, when you are a café selling breakfasts why not offer it all day, surely it is the same as making a mixed grill?

There was never a shortage of places to eat in the old town and most sold good food, if you wanted traditional British food then O'Mara's next to the Babylon was the place to go, meat pies, curries and anything with gravy was always a great hangover cure. I liked the cheap tapas bars where I could get a beer and 5 tapas for 3 euros, great value. I never knew until a Spanish mate told me that the word tapas comes from the saucer-like dish they used to put over your drink to stop the flies. A bit like when they put a slice of lemon in a bottle of Corona, it's not for the taste, just to keep the flies out.

We never bothered with tapas in the Babylon, no point as the brits like a bowl of chips and peanuts. Most of our food was straight out of the freezer and into the deep fat fryer, I wouldn't say it was crap, but it wasn't great. We did try and experiment with better food in the evenings and when I took on Mike the chef, he tried to make the Babylon into a gastropub, this failed miserably, and we went back to the freezer and deep fat fryer. Sometimes you just have to know your customers and give them what they want, let's face it, who doesn't like a big fat burger after a few beers.

As we got into August, I had to close the roof bar during the day as temperatures were crazy. This hurts the business as the bar was a cash cow, it also hurt the staff as they earnt good tips up there, and for anyone thinking of coming to Spain to work in a bar, tips can double your salary; and if you are as good as Alistair or Johnny you can earn more in a day in tips than your salary. I never believed in sharing tips and I insisted that all staff keep their tips, all I asked that they gave something to whoever was working the kitchen. If you are good at what you do and my guys were very good, you know how to work the customers and get the most out of them, I trained them to always go over to a customer when their glass was a third empty and ask if they wanted a refill, also put peanuts out when they are finishing a drink not when they order one. Another trick which helped the guys was I priced bottled beer at 1.80 and in most cases, the customer would throw the 20 cents on the bar, over the day whoever was working would get a lot of 20 cents. Putting pint glasses in the freezer made guys drink them faster, having a bottle of Grey Goose Vodka in the freezer and using oven gloves to serve it always sold more.

One evening I walked into the downstairs bar to pick up some money and in the corner of my eye I spotted a woman sitting on a stool, she was stunning. Whilst I tried to act cool, my mouth dried up and I could feel my heart beating, come on Tony get a grip. She was with a friend who came over and said hello to me and offered her condolences over Ryan. Rose who lived in Benidorm had been to the Babylon a few times with a couple of friends, this time she was with a friend who she had known for 50 years who had come to visit her. The stunning woman turned around and offered her condolences and then told me that her eldest daughter had been close friends with Ryan. Inside I am trying to understand this, best friends with Ryan……….. How?.............. Who was she? How could some random woman on holiday have a daughter who knew Ryan? We exchanged a few pleasantries and I remember Rose asking me what I thought of her friend and I think it was fairly obvious that I liked her. That evening I fell in love.

The following day I was working up on the roof bar and Jane turned up with her youngest daughter Holly who was 17 at the time. They sat down on one of the sofas and I sauntered over trying to keep my composure, this was not normal for me, I had always been easy and relaxed around women. Jane introduced me to Holly, and I said, “you don’t look much like your mother then”, Holly was the spitting image of Jane. Whilst all this was happening the roof was packed and all the gays were waiting in anticipation as to what my next move would be, I came out with what I thought was the worst line in history “when I met you mum I knew I would marry her” ………what the fuck was that?? Did I just say that? Holly responded with “Great, she’s all yours” and then Jane came back with “you can’t have marriage without lunch or dinner”. Well, I thought, I can do that, so I asked Jane out for dinner the following night and she accepted, the whole of the roof bar was in silence. I knew the moment I met Jane that one day she would be my wife.

I booked a beautiful Italian restaurant called Carpe Diem in Altea, a stunning whitewashed small town in the hills outside of Benidorm. I even went to the restaurant in the afternoon to see the manager to make sure we had a good table, something that all guys should do before taking a woman on a first date. I picked Jane up and when we arrived at the restaurant the head waiter recognised me and grabbed a table a stuck on his head and we followed him through the restaurant, I was wondering if the 'all guys should do this' advice was about to fall flat. He plonked the table on the patio with the most amazing views of the mountains, I couldn't have asked for a better position. Throughout the meal, the conversation flowed, and Jane looked even more stunning than when I first met her, she wore a simple contour dress which accentuated her amazing figure, 20 years as a Pilates instructor had obviously paid off. I could not believe my luck when some random guy literally a few feet away from us started playing an acoustic guitar, mellow tunes and so beautiful, I'm sure Jane thought I had organised it. We even ordered the same starter and main course which has to say something, or maybe we just liked the same things to eat.

What really came as a shock was how close she lived in the U.K. to where I used to, she only lived 3 miles away thus how her daughter knew my son. But this is the real kicker……. what are the odds of meeting a woman who is on holiday and in your bar, her daughter was friends with your late son, and you fall in love? I am not a gambling man, but I would think you would have more chance of winning the lottery.

After the meal, I took Jane back to her apartment and I went for a drink, I was shellshocked and needed to understand what was going through my head and heart. I wasn't ready to date, my heart was still desperately painful from losing Ryan and I was still relying on my closest friends to help me get through the day, work helped but they were still a vital part of my life. I also felt guilty for going out on a date, I was meant to be mourning and how could I consider dating at this time, at any time; is there an appropriate time? I have always been mentally strong but like all of us I need a sounding board that Andrew had always been, I would often spill out my anxieties to him over his bar whilst he would sip a glass of rosé, dressed impeccably as always. What I soon realized over the coming weeks is that Jane gave me a reason to get out of bed in the mornings and this helped me more than any bottle of booze.

Jane and I kept in touch through daily texts and calls and even though we weren't seeing each other like most people when they first meet, it felt like a real relationship. It is often said that long-distance relationships don't work, I would argue that it really depends on what commitment you have and how much you want each other. Jane came out again in October and again in the New Year, by this stage she knew everyone in the old town and was becoming a regular face in the bars. They say that beauty is skin deep, and I would say is true, Jane had a remarkable friendly character that reflected her outer beauty; she soon became the agony aunt and mentor to some of the younger guys in the old town.

Whilst I would work in the Babylon, Jane would happily sit up on the roof bar chatting with the locals and tourists and helping out when she could see we were busy. I tried to keep her away from the daily problems around the hotel as I didn't want people to put pressure on her, many tried, but they all failed to use Jane to get to me. It was well known locally that

I had limited patience and fired a lot of people over the years, for me the Babylon was a business, not a democracy or social club and I wasn't going to stand for any nonsense from lazy or dishonest staff. Jane being a kind soul would gently persuade me to change my mind when I had been too harsh. I think there is a lesson here for all women that want their husbands, boyfriends, etc to do something, do not nag them just push the right buttons slowly. I have said ever since I met Jane that she knows what I'm thinking even before I do and I suspect that this is true of most women, they are when it comes to getting things done far smarter than us guys.

As we approached March 2014 jane and I had realized that our relationship was something special, so much so that I had decided to move back to the U.K. so we could be together. Jane would have quite happily moved to Benidorm, but Holly was only 17 and she had yet to finish college and it was only fair that I supported Jane on that. I knew the Babylon would be in good hands as Gladys had been managing it by herself and she had the help of Kai and Alastair who were amazing. So, in March I packed a couple of cases and moved into Jane's house in the U.K.

The first thing I noticed apart from shivering from the cold was how busy everything was, the traffic, people rushing about, and how grey the sky and buildings were. It is a massive culture shock moving back to the U.K. no matter how short a time you have lived abroad, the Spanish way of life was about doing things slowly, eating, drinking, walking, working, etc. One thing I did appreciate however was how efficient everything was, and everything worked, unlike in Spain where modern technology is only applied when it comes to collecting money off you. The Spanish authorities love fining their population for anything and everything, there are no warnings, second chances; you just get fined. Should you decide that you won't pay the fine they will take it directly from your bank account without your consent. The U.K. in comparison has a set of rules, regulations, and a kinder approach to its population, you at least have some regress or an appeal process.

If I'm honest I found the U.K. really difficult for the first few months and I think Jane suspected I wasn't happy. But I knew that there would be some adjustment and I just needed to knuckle down, the added pressure of moving into someone else's home and suddenly having 2 stepdaughters was a lot to absorb. I was fortunate to have considerable experience in the renewable energy sector and secured a job quickly with an American technology company. The money was welcome as the hotel was costing me money with the winter season being particularly harsh and I had huge social security payments to make along with all the salaries and the usual bills. Jane and I were also traveling backward and forwards to Benidorm as I would have occasional meetings with suppliers, lawyers, and had to sort out staffing issues. Life, however, was good and I was getting used to the U.K. and having a local pub made all the difference especially at weekends, we would also go and see Jane's friends in Essex and I still kept in touch with my old mates so managed to get out for a few beers now and again.

The months went quickly, and it was now October 2014 and we were in Benidorm for a few days, Jamie; Jane's oldest daughter was there with her boyfriend and we spent a wonderful few days on the beach and cruising the old town bars in the evenings. One evening we went into Divo Diva which had become one of Jane's favourite bars as she had a great relationship with Andrew and Fritz; Gareth took Jamie outside and he dropped on one knee and popped the question. Andrew is the man of all ceremonies found a big plastic ring behind the bar and gave it to Gareth, so he put something on Jamie's finger, we all got very pissed that night and the two of them tied the knot the following year in Cyprus. Jane and I had also moved into a new apartment down Poniente with a stunning sea view, we needed somewhere that was ours rather than just mine.

As 2014 went into 2015 we had been backward and forwards many times and thoughts were turning to moving back out to Benidorm when the time was right, Holly still was the priority and she had started working. We went back out to Benidorm on the 12th of February and as per usual I got tied up in various bits with the Babylon, the electrical issues in the building were so bad that I had to get my lawyers to write a letter to the landlord demanding that the issues are fixed, or I would withhold the rent. The following evening, we had some wonderful tapas in Cava Aragonesa and ended up in Divo Diva around 11.30 pm. Jane was chatting with Andrew, she turned around and there I was on one knee asking her to marry me. She burst into tears which initially worried me as I thought most women would be happy with a proposal of marriage, thankfully she said yes and Andrew on cue brought out the now-famous plastic ring. I still say to this day that I was tying my shoelaces and it wasn't a marriage proposal, of course, the now Mrs. H is smarter than that. The only people that knew of my intended proposal were Rose, Jane's friend who introduced us, Jamie, and Andrew. Rose had been calling and texting me relentlessly all evening asking if I have done it.

Word got around the old town like wildfire and it was a wonderful night celebrating our engagement with our closest friends. Not long after we set a date for May 18th, 2017.

Chapter 12

On May 16th, 2017 Jane and I were married at the Weybridge registry office in Surrey, present was my best man, family, and close friends. But this wasn't and still isn't our wedding anniversary, we both decided that we wanted a formal blessing in Spain on the 18th just 2 days later. Our good friends at Papagayo, Juri, and Mario had offered to host the wedding at their bar with La Rana one of the oldest Spanish restaurants in Benidorm providing the food. Both are located on these beautiful Spanish steps flanked by palm trees and insight of the 300-year-old San Jaime church, it is a stunningly beautiful and romantic setting.

Remarkably, the blessing was easy to organise and we found a lovely Spanish pastor who would perform the ceremony in both Spanish and English, we wanted it to feel authentic and also respect those Spanish friends who were coming. We visited La Rana a couple of times and settled on a buffet that would include all their house specialties and a few other dishes which were uniquely Spanish. As a family-run business, they made us feel special and we still eat there now, the food is amazing, and you are made to feel like one of the family. The boys in Papagayo were getting a little nervous especially when we told them that there would be around 150 people, no pressure then.

Our great friends Nino and Flavio at Italian Twist offered to make the cake and having seen some of their previous creations Jane jumped at the offer, she settled on a huge book with a few beautiful words written in icing on the cover. Those that were asked to be part of the preparations were all known to Jane and me, this made the whole thing more special, rather than having strangers we had friends who were not just contributors they were part of our happiness. An old mate of mine from the new town was asked to provide the photography, Irish Mike the biker who would normally be dressed in leathers and snapping tourists happily agreed. We had originally asked some performers in the new town to provide live music, but they had some real 'diva' moments wanting stages and full-blown sound systems, so we settled in the end for a Dutch guy called the 'Voice' who was a good friend of Juri and Mario.

The one thing that Jane and I were both adamant about was that the blessing and party would be informal and fun. We didn't want formal dining, nor did we want our friends spread out and isolated from each other, this is not how things are done in the old town and we wanted it to be a celebration of marriage and friendship. Too often I have been to weddings and you are stuck on a table for hours with boring people talking about boring things and for me it is torture. The whole seating plan consisted of around 30 chairs for close family and those that needed to sit, everyone else was asked to stand on the steps and look down as the blessing took place.

I am not an expert on women's dresses, especially wedding dresses so I can't elaborate too much on Jane's dress. I know you, girls, like specifics but all I can say is it was a full-length 'one-off 'gown with sparkly things in a light peach colour.

Jane obviously looked stunning, and on the day, it shimmered in the afternoon sun. Oddly, a year after we were married Jane noticed some reality TV star wearing the same dress in some social media post, sadly for this reality star she had neither the finesse, class nor sophistication of Jane. Holly and Jamie were the bridesmaids and Bradley my other son was an unofficial usher, as the ceremony was less formal there wasn't a real need to show people to their seats, bums sat where the name tag told them too.

When the day came and all was ready my nerves really kicked in and thankfully, I had Gareth, Josh who is Holly's boyfriend, and Bradley there to ply me with large G&Ts to soften my anxiety. As this was one of life's big moments a little Dutch courage was required, obviously not too much as I am well known as a lightweight when it comes to alcohol. The irony of those that were helping us dawned on me, Dutch Bar owners, Dutch singer, Italian cake bakers, Irish biker photographer, and of course the Spanish catering and Pastor. This diversity really reflected the old town, and I was proud to have such a mixed bunch being part of our special day.

30 minutes before Jane was due to arrive my anxiety levels were going through the roof, only 15 people had turned up and this could be a disaster. Thankfully within 15 minutes, the place was packed, those that needed a seat were sat, there were people down the edges of the steps, the middle needed to be kept clear for Jane to walk down. The sun was shining, the sky was a beautiful clear deep blue, not a cloud to be seen. All we needed now was the future, Mrs. H, to turn up,

thankfully I had no worries about her having second thoughts as we were already officially married.

Jane arrived at 4 pm on the dot and was accompanied by Rose, her oldest friend there to give her away. Jane had sadly lost her mother when she was 19 and her father was too frail to make the wedding. She had choreographed the entry perfectly, Jamie and Holly set a slow but graceful pace navigating the cobbled steps, Jane with Rose by her side was right behind them followed by Mario and Juri dressed in vibrant pink suits. I was waiting for Jane at the bottom of the steps standing by a small simple rectangular table decorated with flowers. Next to the table was another smaller one with 3 photos, one of my son Ryan, one of Rose's late partner Ron who was like a father to Jane, and one of Jane's mother. Ron had died the same time as Ryan and I remember looking at those photos and felt we both had everyone there, we were complete. Standing next to me was my best man Wayne.

Wayne and I have been good friends for many years, we have both shared the joys, pain, and frustrations that life thrusts upon us; divorce, the birth of our children, and the loss of those closest to us.

The Pastor started the blessing, and we were joined by many onlookers and locals leaning over their balconies, I felt so humbled to be part of that community and my earlier anxiety had now been replaced by a deep sense of happiness. The blessing was simple and touched us all, bizarrely as the Pastor finished his final words a small cloud appeared over Jane and me, and a few drops of rain fell on Jane and me, then the cloud moved on as quick as it came. We were stunned and for a few seconds everything stopped as everyone looked up at the now clear blue sky, the locals were making the sign of the cross and the Pastor looked at us and said: "they are the tears of God blessing you". Words then and even now fail me, was this divine intervention at work?

We celebrated with all our friends and family for the rest of the evening and it was amazing. Everyone had got the simple ceremony request and come dressed in Hawaiian shirts, pinks, oranges, and other vibrant colours. The music was cheesy and perfect and thank god we followed Papagayo's advice and went with the 'Voice', you know when a singer understands the crowd and sings old classics that gets the party going. When Nino and Flavio walked down the steps with the cake the Voice knew the perfect song to accompany the occasion, within seconds 150 guests and all those hanging off balconies sang the words "When the moon hits your eye like a big pizza pie, that's amore", it was beautiful and incredibly moving. Our Italian friends responded with a swagger befitting Dean Martin's classic song and the cake made it to the table in one piece.

As we had a free bar and the food was a help-yourself buffet people mingled and chatted freely, most were pissed but you see everyone was relaxed. I started chatting with a couple who were sitting on their own, they seemed nice and they said they were good friends with the groom. Shortly afterward I asked Wayne to chuck them out, I had no idea who they were considering they were good friends of mine, you must admire the cheek of wedding crashers.

Jane and I decided to leave the reception around 10 pm and headed over to Brief Encounter where we could relax and get some breathing space, it had been a long and tiring day. Over the next few hours, we bumped into most of the guests in the various bars in the old town, and by 2 am we were completely shattered and pissed home time. We had discussed having a honeymoon in the Caribbean and fancied Guadeloupe, this was where the TV program 'Death in Paradise' was located, and we wanted to stay in the same town where it was filmed. However, after some discussion we realized that the only place both of us really wanted to be was right here in Benidorm with our friends and family, so we stayed and had a wonderful week.

The months that followed weren't much different than those that preceded, we got back to our lives in the U.K. and the Babylon continued to run under Gladys's stewardship along with Alistair, Kai, and the others. I was offered a job-based in Porto which I accepted, the role, however, involved extensive travel and for the next couple of years, I worked with Governments on building and restoring power to conflict zones and deprived areas. Having the opportunity to travel to amazing places was a real treat, meeting locals and helping them to have a future where power would change their lives was a real privilege.

I know Jane worried as many of these places had been or were still on the news and it was strictly off-limits to tourists because of the danger, I fortunately always had an armed security detail and a bulletproof vest, so I felt safe. Having a gun pointed at you at checkpoints is not detailed in most job descriptions but it never worried me. I was stopped by 2 very heavily armed soldiers at a checkpoint in the middle east who were very suspicious and asked me a lot of questions and studied my passport with real intensity, whilst this was happening I was standing very still with my arms raised and looking at the floor. Then one of them looked at me and said 2 words which sent shivers down my back "Manchester United" .... Did he just say, "Manchester United"!!! It seems that football is the global icebreaker and the mood changed instantly and whilst I am a Chelsea supporter I was not going to argue with my new best friends.

The one thing that I realized very quickly is that what you see on the news, read in papers, and see on social media is nothing near the truth. In Colombia I was met with warmth and respect, at no time did I see gun-toting militias or drug cartels shooting up streets from the back of a Toyota Hilux, I think the western media likes to portray Colombia in a permanently negative light. Bogota was a very cosmopolitan, sophisticated city with a real European feel, it is still my favourite capital city in the world, and I would recommend it to anyone. In Bogota, the only thing you must be wary of is the altitude which can really affect your drinking, I was floating like a fairy after 2 beers.

Whilst Colombia and Bogota were amazing, Rio de Janeiro in Brazil was one of the frightening cities I have ever been to. Advertised as a glamourous tropical paradise in travel brochures it is a shithole which is riddled with crime and is unbelievably filthy, when I was there 2 tourists were robbed and murdered. Surrounding Rio are shanty towns called

'Favela's' which house desperate and poor locals but there are also some very nasty and dangerous criminals who descend on Rio at night hunting tourists for money and valuables.

Often, I would see complete contrasts, take Cairo and Tokyo as an example. Occasionally, I had to negotiate deals with major investment funds that thankfully weren't located in warzones. When Frank Sinatra sang "New York is the city that never sleeps", he obviously never spent any time in Cairo which is the nosiest, dustiest, and the craziest city I have ever stayed in. My first time there I stayed in the Radisson in Heliopolis; I didn't sleep for 4 days, drivers in Egypt have their hands permanently attached to their horns. The next time I checked into the Hilton, which was away from any hooting and busy roads, the one thing however I could not get away from was the shits which is all part of the Cairo experience. Food in Egypt is truly awful, and I defy anyone to eat the local food and not spend the next few days on the toilet. In contrast, Tokyo is the cleanest, most efficient city I have ever been to. Nobody drops litter and if there is an odd crisp packet or wrapper flying around the police will pick it up immediately and put it in their pocket, you will be hard-pressed to find any litter bins in Tokyo. If you smoke then you will be asked to go inside a restaurant or bar, it is not permitted in the streets unless you are in an authorised smoking area. Everything is incredibly efficient and spotless; people are polite, and the city is virtually crime-free. My favourite thing in Tokyo, these wonderful steamed white buns with pork meat inside them, they were so yummy.

Food is a fantastic way of engaging and getting to know people and whilst I suffered from the shits in Egypt and other countries this was more down to minerals in water and other gastric issues that affect most tourists. I have eaten some strange and bizarre dishes and have been treated to some delicacies which would make most people vomit at the very thought. I was honoured and humbled when served a sheep's head whilst in the middle of nowhere on the Syrian Jordanian border, a house specialty which was served with rice and covered in sour fermented yogurt. The whole meal is eaten with your hands except the eyeball where a long spoon is provided to prize it out, it is a strange sensation when an eyeball pops in your mouth. After this meal, I was honoured to be taken around one of the oldest mosques in Jordan and witness my friend take evening prayer.

In Brazil I had a very nice stew with a cow's tongue poking out the top, in Asia I ate locusts on a stick, and I have eaten various fish which look prehistoric, all of these meals were with wonderful people and I was proud to be part of their culture and traditions.

One thing that used to drive me crazy, especially when if you are a business traveller and often stay in very luxurious hotels are the constant approaches by prostitutes when you are sat at the bar. These are not the common garden variety you see on the streets, rather extremely high class and expensive professionals who can charge upwards of $5,000 an hour. I was propositioned more times than I would care for and after a while, I just get used to it, although I used to get annoyed at the more persistent ladies. At the lower end and a lot more disturbing are the ones that hang around bars and cafes looking for their next punter. One time I was sitting having a coffee in a café near my hotel in São Paulo when I noticed a woman and her daughter staring at me, the girl must have been no older than 16; the mother leaned over and pointed at her daughter and asked me in broken English if I liked her daughter. I knew exactly where this was going and I beat a hasty retreat to the safety and sanctity of my hotel pool where I had a cold beer and I telephoned Jane. Such is the desperation and poverty that families face in the poorer parts of South America, they sell off their daughters for prostitution or even marriage to older men.

I always had to be careful when traveling to dangerous countries where kidnapping was a real problem. Many business travellers are taken and ransomed for hundreds of thousands of pounds, most are returned without harm when their company's pay the ransom; some are never returned at all. I used to take off my wedding ring and tan the ring line before any journey to a dangerous country, showing that you have a wife or husband is not a good idea. I did not shave for a few days and always took old clothes and tried to blend in with the locals as much as possible, for me having blue eyes meant that sunglasses were compulsory. Luckily, I never witnessed or experienced any problems, but I know of people that have been kidnapped and thankfully they lived to tell the tale.

In addition to having guns pointed at me, the real threat of being kidnapped and constantly having the shits, the only other issue I had to contend with was insects, snakes, spiders, and anything else that wanted to eat me. I had all the necessary inoculations for hepatitis A, hepatitis B, typhoid, cholera, yellow fever, and rabies but when traveling into the Amazon rain forest I was more concerned with bloody great big snakes and scary-looking insects that looked like flying cupcakes. We were kitted out with snake gaiters and wore mosquito repellent clothes, but I was always aware that some huge boa constrictor might be eyeing me up for its next meal. I was lucky, in all of my travels I only got bitten by a spider which made my finger swell up like a Cumberland sausage but thankfully went down after a couple of days and I was left with a black hole for a few weeks.

Whilst I was traveling the Babylon continued to function and despite the distance, I kept in touch and the guys had a good grip on things. The last few years had been eventful if not tragic but meeting and marrying Jane softened the pain that I felt after losing Ryan. I think you really have to live life to experience life, being safe and never taking a chance will always be a safe option but it will never give you the sights, sounds, smells, and thrills that the world has to offer. If I had never moved to Benidorm and bought the hotel I would never have met Jane, losing Ryan destroyed me and it will forever fill my heart with pain but love always triumphs suffering and my memories and love for Ryan will always be there, in my heart and soul. My other son Bradley has matured into a good decent man, he has integrity and honour; a father can ask nothing more of his son and I am deeply proud of him. Being married to Jane and suddenly becoming a stepfather to 2 beautiful intelligent girls enriched my life and it taught me new things; I am now an expert in false eyelashes, false nails, pouting selfies, and the Kardashian's.

So, what happened to the Babylon? Well, next time you are in Benidorm, pop into the Babylon Bar and ask for Mr. H and I will tell you.

Printed in Great Britain
by Amazon

16733891R00080